THE OFFER

THE OFFER

A GUIDE TO THE RICHES OF KING SOLOMON

ROLAND WIEDERAENDERS, ESQ.

Published by

QUETZALHILOCO PUBLISHING CO.

Austin, Texas

www.thchalm.com

Copyright 2020 by QuetzalHiloco Publishing Co.

Cover Design: Sam Radue, Austin, Texas

Center figure illustration from Eliphas Levi's *Histoire de la magie* (*The History of Magic*) originally published in 1860

Also from QuetzalHiloco:

Le Club Des Hashischins:
An Expressive Transliteration,

and from our Inno¢ent Books imprint:

Rhyming Psalms

Rhyming Job

Rhyming Solomon

Rhyming Matthew

This book is dedicated to my mom, Mrs. Laura Dinda, and my dad, Mr. Roland Wiederaenders, II, with much love.

Let them, your father, mother both be glad,
let her who bore you, much rejoicing, have.

--T. H. Chalm's Rhyming Proverbs 23:25

"Sous ses lois l'Amour veut qu'on jouisse / D'un bonheur qui jamais ne finesse."

(Love wishes that everyone enjoy unending happiness under his laws.)

--From Jean Galbert de Campistron's libretto of Jean-Baptiste Lully's 1686 opera, Acis et Galatée

CONTENTS

1	INTRODUCTION	1
2	THE BIBLE STUDY	8
3	THE OFFER	16
4	THE TASK	18
5	THE TASK—WHO AM I?	25
6	THE TASK—WHAT DO YOU WANT?	38
7	THE TASK—HOW CAN I BEST SERVE?	52
8	THE TASK—YOUR HOURLY RATE	73
9	THE WAGER—PART 1	77
10	THE WAGER—PART 2	81
11	TRAUMA AND PSYCHEDELICS	83
12	YOUR FOCUS—AN ILLUSTRATION FROM FREEDIVING	103
13	COMMUNITY AND WANTS—HORSE FORCE MULTIPLIER ILLUSTRATION	109
14	REST—ILLUSTRATIONS FROM MATERIAL POSSESSIONS; TITLES; POSITIONS	116
15	MEDITATION—PART 1	129

16	MEDITATION—PART 2	148
17	HUMILITY	158
18	DIET AND WELLNESS	165
19	THINK AND GROW RICH	173
20	EDUCATION AND THE SCOPE OF AMBITION/SERVICE	190
21	ENJOY YOUR TOIL—ACCEPTANCE	198
22	BOBBY MCGEE AND FREEDOM	208
23	MODERN AMERICAN CHRISTIANITY— PART 1	217
24	MODERN AMERICAN CHRISTIANITY— PART 2	224
25	REAL ESTATE AND LEVERAGED RETURNS	240
26	FEDERAL INCOME TAX PLANNING	256
27	OTHER INVESTMENTS AND SERVICES	278
28	CONCLUSION	280

APPENDIX—PSYCHEDELIC BIBLIOGRAPHY

THE OFFER

A BLESSING OR A CURSE, FROM TIME TO TIME,
WHO'S RICH IS WHAT THE UNIVERSE DECIDES.
YOU'RE BLESSED IF YOU, ENJOYMENT, HAVE, WITH LIFE.
AND IN YOUR EARTHLY TOIL, FULFILLMENT, FIND.
THE OFFER IS THE TASK FOR YOU TO WRITE.
I'LL PAY YOUR RATE FOR FIVE HOURS WITHOUT RISK,
THESE QUESTIONS, THREE THAT YOU, YOURSELF, SHOULD ASK
SO YOU WILL KNOW HOW TO ENJOY YOUR WEALTH
(TRANSPARENT HONESTY WILL SERVE YOU WELL):
WHO ARE YOU? WHAT ARE YOUR DESIRES, FOR SURE?
DESCRIBE HOW IS IT THAT YOU BEST CAN SERVE?
WRITE DOWN YOUR ANSWERS ON SOME PAGES, FEW
AND IF YOU MAKE THE WAGER, OUR YEAR'S QUEUE,
INVESTMENT PLANNING, YOU WILL ENTER IN.
THE TASK AND ALL YOUR THOUGHTS, WE'LL HELP EXPAND.
THROUGHOUT THAT TIME OUR TEAM WILL WORK WITH YOU
TO BRING, THE THINGS YOU WROTE, A NEW LIGHT, TO.
THOSE PEOPLE, POOR OR RICH, WHO STILL ENJOY,
THE WEALTH THEY HAVE, WITH WISDOM, THEY DEPLOY.
THEY MAY BE CLIENTS, BUT FOR SURE, ARE FRIENDS,
THE SIMPLE TRUTHS THAT THEY ALL UNDERSTAND:
HOW THEY WILL EVERY DAY, THEIR BLESSINGS, COUNT.
TO HEAVEN THEY GIVE CREDIT WITH A SHOUT.
BUT OTHERS WHOM THEY LOVE LIVE IN DESPAIR.
OUR COUNSEL CAN WORK TO LAY PROBLEMS BARE.
IF YOU WOULD KNOW THE CONTENTS OF MY THOUGHTS,
THE WAGER THAT YOU MAKE WON'T RISK A LOT.
THE PRICE HAS SEVERAL ZEROS BY THE DOT,
BUT MONEY IS, A HURDLE TO THIS, NOT.
IF YOU'RE MY FRIEND, I'LL MAKE A GUARANTEE,
I'LL GIVE YOU MY FIVE HOURS OF TALK FOR FREE.
OUR RATES, IF YOURS IS HIGHER, MUCH, BY FAR,
OUR BUDGET, MARKETING, WON'T REACH THE STARS,
BUT THIS, THE WAY, THE WAGER, WE WILL MAKE,
WHEN WE AT PRESENT CAN'T PAY SUCH A RATE.
YOUR FAVORITE CHARITY, IF YOU'RE BILL GATES,
I'LL DONATE CASH, FIVE TIMES *MY* HOURLY RATE.
IF BILL WOULD KNOW THE CONTENTS OF MY THOUGHTS,
THEN HE DECIDES THE NUMBER OF THE NAUGHTS.

Chapter 1

Introduction

I write in this book a lot about my ambition from an early age to be a creative writer. For the last few years, I have focused my creative writing exclusively on poetry and since 2017, I wrote a total of six books of poetry. I have another on the way. I describe my poetry and its essential importance to this book in later chapters.

While not many people have read my poetry, my ambition with writing always expresses as a desire to write something that everyone can connect with quickly. Maybe people can connect with The Offer more readily than my poetry? If that is the case, I may be headed in the right direction. If I sold millions of copies of The Offer and it caused me to grow my new investment adviser firm, Real Advisers, that would work to my great economic advantage!

One of the reasons I wrote The Offer was to tell you about my new company, a Texas-registered investment adviser, Real Advisers LLC RIA Series (CRD #302991). I also must let you know where you can find more information about Real Advisers. We are temporarily housing our Form ADV Part 2 at my publishing company's website (thchalm.com). This document provides required narrative disclosure regarding our business as a Texas-registered investment adviser focusing on representing financial advisory clients who want to acquire and grow wealth, provided that they want to allocate a greater-than-average portion of their portfolio to active and passive investments in residential and commercial real estate. These real estate investments generally would be in assets other than REITs offered in the public equities markets, but the investments we recommend could include those. Our primary emphasis is advising people with direct investments in real estate and investments in privately syndicated residential and commercial real estate assets.

Would it make this book more appealing if I told you that contained within its pages is a business concept that you could use to grow your investment advisory practice in a way so that your clients' wealth increases at a rate you've never seen?

If you have never worked as an investment adviser before or don't even know what I am talking about, this book focuses on two things: wealth and how to enjoy it. These two things are the most important things that an investment adviser needs to understand about his or her client. The Offer is a business model that you can use in your practice to grow whether you are affiliated with Real Advisers or not.

Would this book be more attractive to you if I said you could use it as a guide for going down the path of your own wealth creation and accumulation? You can use The Offer to help you grow your personal wealth even if you do not want to be an investment adviser. I may not ever pay you The Offer Price, but through this book, I can give you the guidance to work the magic of The Offer on your own.

You can use this book to grow any business. You will be able to use the tools that I am giving you to accelerate your growth in any field in a way that will connect you more with your core values.

I wrote The Offer to provide you with a tool that you could take and figure out answers to problems that people pay me thousands of dollars to spend hours and hours to figure out for them. This book is intended to be a tool to help you think for yourself, literally.

You will hear a lot about meditation in this book. If that scares you, I understand. I did not connect with meditation until three years ago during my mid-40s. I can tell you why I had a hard time connecting with meditation, and also what to do about it IF you still want to try this ancient practice despite any apprehension that you may feel. This is a not a cult and I am not trying to convert you. I am recommending meditation in this book as a practice similar to the practice of yoga. Meditation is yoga for your mind.

I am hoping that you will read this book and want so much to hear what I have to say about your financial and life circumstances that you will pay me my hourly rate to do that. That is only one way that my firm makes money, but by accepting The Wager, that is how we gain many of our clients.

The central concepts of this book are simple:

- A short Bible study that does not require you to believe in God;

- The three questions of The Task that are very short but that will require a long time (maybe the rest of your life) for you to answer fully and consistently with your true identity and desires, and in a way that best serves your community; and

- One proposition about a fundamental need that we all have, a place to live, and how Real Advisers' investment advisory practice focuses on helping people meet that need in a way so that the place they live can be an investment tool.

Real Advisers focuses on real estate because, on average, investing in leveraged real estate will allow you to achieve the highest risk adjusted returns (measured by the Sharpe ratio, an investment management tool that measures potential investment returns of various asset classes against their relative risks).

Like the classic, Think and Grow Rich, if you understand these concepts and know how to employ them to help you grow wealthy, you can stop reading this book immediately. If you would be interested in knowing my insights about these ideas, and how I answered the questions of The Task in my own life, read on. The rest of the book is about how these concepts are illustrated in my life and led me to create Real Advisers.

For you to participate in The Offer, ideally, I already have some knowledge of who you are and what your priorities are. It is not necessary, but it can be helpful and will make my sales pitch even more powerful. Knowledge is power.

For anyone who wants to accept The Offer, to describe The Offer to you and how it works, first, I must know your hourly rate. Everyone who must work for someone else to feed themselves has an hourly rate. Imagine this to be the best hourly rate that you ever earned. When we go through this exercise, please allow me to challenge you in this area, but what I usually find is that most people vastly undervalue their time. You have infinite value and potential even if you do not feel like it, so your rate really is equal to Bill Gates'. This is the case even though you may not see it and/or the world does not yet recognize it. One of the arguments in this book is that the universe recognizes your infinite value, and that is why you exist. If you immediately think what you just read is unacceptable tautology, this book may not be for you. If you do not know what a tautology is, read on.

If you do not have to work, you may not be an ideal client for the firm, but you still may. To determine whether you are an ideal candidate, ask yourself whether you know what the blessing of wealth is? It is a simple answer that you probably already know, and I have already written it in the preceding pages. In fact, the answer is the entire premise of this book.

If you do not think you know the answer, you really do. It may be just that you do not know that you know, or maybe you have forgotten.

The true blessing of wealth is to have wealth and the ability to enjoy it. Do you have wealth? Do you enjoy it? Many people have little cash but massive life enjoyment, and many people have lots of cash but are miserable? Where are you?

Put a check in the box that applies to you:

	Rich	Poor
Happy		
Sad		

If your hourly rate is higher than mine ($1,000 per hour in the financial advisory practice, minimum five hours), then you may not be an ideal client candidate for Real Advisers, but you still may. Nevertheless, you probably know someone in your life with access to great wealth, but they still are unhappy. We think we can help that person with The Offer.

Chapter 2
The Bible Study

The entire premise of The Offer is a passage from the Old Testament of the Bible, the source text of my personal belief system, Christianity. When I refer to my "source text" in this book, I am talking about the Bible. I suspect that you have heard of this text before and probably even have seen one in the drawer by your hotel bed.

The Old Testament of the Bible includes five books of poetry: Psalms; Proverbs; Ecclesiastes; Job; and Song of Solomon. I have spent a great deal of time with these books of the Bible in other creative endeavors through my "T. H. Chalm" poetry. My publishing company, QuetzalHiloco, has self-published these books through Amazon and KDP. Please note, total sales of these works are extremely low, but I want to sell many more copies of The Offer!

The Chalm poetry for The Offer directly came from Ecclesiastes, in the 19th verse of its fifth chapter. Chalm wrote a rhyming version of the entire book of Ecclesiastes in iambic pentameter, and his "rendition" of this specific verse follows:

> To all whom God gives both possessions, wealth,
> and likewise, whom he has enabled well
> to find enjoyment, to accept their lot
> in all their toils, this is the gift of God.

What these verses assert is that the universe controls who is wealthy and who is not. Alternatively, you could say at least that there is not a direct correlation between hard work and all the attributes that tend to be predictors of high earning potential and actual wealth since we all know stories of brilliant, industrious people who struggle financially, and we all know or are aware of lazy idiots that somehow are fabulously wealthy.

We also know about people who are rich and miserable, and we know people (maybe) who are poor but happy.

I am using the word "Bible" specifically to trigger readers. It triggers people on both sides, in the sense that Christians gravitate toward the word since the Bible is their (our) holy book. People who have a negative perception of Christians (because of the evils done in the name of Jesus) see the word "Bible" and maybe roll their eyes or even stick out their tongues in disgust when they read the word or hear it spoken. That's OK! As a for-profit enterprise seeking to help all of humanity, we believe that Real Advisers can work with people of different faiths, including people that have extremely negative perceptions of Christians and Christianity. All that is required for The Offer is for you to at least *somewhat* identify with our ecumenical, non-denominational, irreligious "Bible Study", and recognize quickly the qualifier that belief in God is not necessary. You can just believe in the universe instead, or pick your own goddess or god.

Here is "The Bible Study":

- The universe decides who is rich and who is poor. We all know poor, hardworking geniuses and lazy dolts who somehow are wealthy. We have to admit that there is an element of unpredictability as to who is wealthy and who isn't, and most wealthy people (measured by dollars) will admit that they became wealthy only because they happened to be at the right place at the right time.

- Wealth is either a blessing or a curse, but it isn't necessarily one or the other. We all know happy and engaged people who don't have a lot of money, and at least have heard stories about rich people who are miserable and isolated (even if you don't actually know such a person). Which one would you rather be?

- Wealth is a blessing only if you both possess it and know how to enjoy it.

Can you disagree?

I note that a small percentage of the people reading this will get hung up on some of the specific language. The Bible Study requires you to engage in a high-level thought exercise where you may need to suspend temporarily some of your normal ways of thinking.

I note too that some people get hung up on the notion that their free will might be excluded, or that because the universe controls all things, I no longer am responsible for directing my will. I am not saying that we do not have absolute agency (free will), or that we are not responsible for our actions. At the same time, I do not know that anyone can disagree with the notion that if the universe either intends something to happen or not, nothing happens outside of its intention. So, I can have my free will but there is another force at work.

This "other force" at work does not necessarily

give me apprehension. My belief system and my experiences with psilocybin and Ayahuasca strongly reinforced the notion that the force of the universe is a benevolent one and it has specific knowledge of me. I perceive now in a way I wasn't able to before that somehow I am part of the infinitesimally intricate design of the universe. I discuss psychedelics and their relevance to The Offer beginning in Chapter 5 (entitled "Who Am I?") and elsewhere in this book.

If you get hung up on the term, "the universe", then replace that with "God", or vice versa. As an alternative to both, you could say that there is no direct scientific correlation that works in every instance where you can measure by personality characteristics and opportunity whether someone is going to be wealthy (and if so whether they will be able to enjoy their wealth). There is a "something else" that enables them to achieve wealth, first, and then to enjoy it, second.

I have identified a key tool, an ancient technology, practice, and method that you can employ to direct your thoughts and will. This is a practice you can learn in a few minutes, but that you can use for the rest of your life to your benefit. This tool is meditation. If this makes you nervous, don't worry. Meditation can be learned very easily, and I can teach you how. In fact, we can meditate together in a few minutes.

I must be faithful to explain my belief system since I am invoking my ancient source text as a place of authority in these matters. Our text illustrates universal truths that apply to everyone no matter what their specific beliefs are.

My source text drives me to who I perceive as the supreme divine ruler and authority of the universe, and I frequently appeal to that authority to intervene on my behalf. A prayer taught to me by that supreme divine authority in the Gospel of Matthew includes my daily personal pledge of allegiance to my deity's will, consistent with the ancient hermetic maxim: AS ABOVE, SO BELOW. The prayer that Jesus instructs is "Not my will, but thine be done." This represents a fundamental opportunity for everyone reading this book.

I don't want to tell you that you must believe in Jesus to be saved. The reason I don't want to tell you that is because it's not up to me who goes to the Christian heaven. The reason I do not want to tell you that must believe in Jesus is not because I do not believe in Jesus or do not want you to. I do, but only in the sense that I want everyone to be connected to what I perceive as the ultimate source of love in the universe. Nevertheless, I understand that it may be impossible for you to see this because you might believe differently than me. Telling people they better do what you say, or think what you think or else they're going to hell is psychotic and will never allow you to make friends with the people I want to be friends with.

So, I believe in Jesus and would encourage you to do the same. There are much better evangelists and apologists than me though. I would direct all skeptics to the works of C. S. Lewis as one of the greatest apologists of the 20th century, and particularly to his book, Mere Christianity. If you reject Christianity after reading what he wrote, I truly will respect your intelligence and would be curious about your reasoning. It certainly would influence my thinking.

If you have another belief system, please recommend to me those important texts that best illustrate its most crucial aspects.

I respect other people's beliefs. 99.9% of the people in the world can work together regardless of their beliefs to attempt to end the problems of hate, hunger, homelessness, and poverty. When those problems are completely solved, please spend as much of your time and energy as you want arguing about religion. Argument over fine points of theology, even if they reflect truths that you hold as irrevocable, inviolable, and universal, rarely accomplishes anything.

What is it that you really want? Do you want peace? Don't argue. If you want to be wealthy, you must have peace and rest. That is the case because industriousness is a strong predictor of long-term economic success. If you don't know how to rest, you cannot work hard.

What is it that you want? Do you really want wealth? What does heart-centered wealth mean to you? These questions are expressed in The Task. Before we get to The Task, however, I must first briefly describe "The Offer".

Chapter 3

The Offer

The Offer is simple: I will pay you for five hours of your time at your hourly rate, unconditionally, to answer the questions of The Task for yourself. When you perform The Task, you will be working at a thought problem that may take you the rest of your life to answer. It will work to your economic advantage and long-term growth potential to answer the questions of The Task now, and to keep asking them about yourself for the rest of your life. I am going to do the same.

When The Offer is made, in exchange for your mere agreement to answer the questions of The Task, the offeror pays "The Offer Price". You will have to create a user profile, join the Real Advisers network (no need to enter a credit card), and provide us with some demographic information that we will agree to hold confidentially. You agree to provide responses to the questions of The Task to help us determine whether you would be an ideal client or partner. A thoughtful and detailed written response would be most helpful. Nevertheless, even if you never give us your response, you still get to keep The Offer Price.

There are some people who will be so skeptical, they will not even accept The Offer Price, thinking that there is some scam or hidden agenda. There is a hidden agenda (and I discuss it throughout this book), but one that is designed intentionally to advance simultaneously the combined interests of Real Advisers and our clients.

Chapter 4
The Task

Answering the three questions of The Task is necessary for you to take action and make sure your thinking is directed on a course that will best serve your long-term financial best interests. Go and answer the questions of The Task and come back when you have spent five hours. These hours can include time in the shower and while you are driving to the grocery store or work (if you still drive to your job).

These questions are not original to me, but they are so simple, I do not think that they could be copyright protected. "The Offer" for you to accept is that I will unconditionally pay you for five hours of your time to answer the three questions of The Task for yourself, where your answers will help you financially and trend you in the direction of achieving true heart-centered wealth. The questions are:

- Who are you?
- What do you want?
- How can you serve?

Here is the section regarding The Task from my poem, The Offer:

These questions, three, that you should ask yourself
so you will know how to enjoy your wealth
(transparent honesty will serve you well):
Who are you? What are your desires, for sure?
Describe how is it that you best can serve?

I believe I first heard these questions (Who am I? What do I want? How can I best serve?) about two years ago in class from my yoga instructor, Jennifer Turner (who recently got her real estate agent's license). When I heard them, I started thinking about their profound simplicity.

The answers to these questions encompass all of the knowledge that we need to trend ourselves in the direction of creating heart-centered long-term economic success and wealth accumulation.

If you do not know the answers to these questions, you will apply your energy in a haphazard way. This is the case because you will be acting without self-knowledge. Without that self-knowledge, you don't know what it is that you really want? Do you want to be a golfer because you think that's the only way to really get ahead in life, or do you want to be a golfer because you really enjoy the sport?

Who are you? What is at the core of your identity? My belief system informs me of a fact that has the deepest significance for The Offer. As a being with a specific identity, I perceive that I possess an eternal durability and special significance to the universe both in my life and also even after death. I believe that there is an existence after death where there is some sort of continuity between what we are experiencing now and whatever "life" follows. In my belief system, this life after death is called the "resurrection". The Gospel stories inform us of a Jesus who came back from the dead with the ability to walk through walls, appear and disappear instantaneously, and otherwise behave as some sort of God-man, an immortal being with powers even exceeding the miraculous ones described in the stories about his life before his crucifixion. I believe I will receive a similar glorified and eternal body somehow and at some time after my death. I admit that I am uncertain about the specifics.

The exact details about the eternal being or personage that I will inhabit for eternity are unknown to me now. I understand from my source text that there is supposed to be a "ministry of reconciliation", where all the things that appear broken now will be made new, and that we have will have mansions prepared for us in heaven. I'm OK with living in a mansion. Honestly, I could be happy in an apartment as long as I have quick access to a sunny beach. You can have my mansion in the snowy mountains of heaven if that would be your dream place to live. Give me the beach.

There are multiple passages in the Bible about how God is our provider. The most famous is Psalm 23:

> The LORD, my shepherd, is, I, nothing, lack.
> Me, downwards lie in pastures, green, he makes.
> The quiet waters, he leads me beside,
> my soul refreshed. Along the paths, those right,
> he guides me for his name's sake. Though I walk
> the valley, through it, e'en that one most dark,
> I will no evil, fear, for you're with me;
> your rod and staff are comforting to me.
> Before me, there, a table, you prepare,
> my enemies, a place where they're aware.
> My head with oil, anoint, that's what you do;
> it overflows, my cup. For surely, your
> love, goodness, both of them will, me, pursue
> all of the days of my life, and I will,
> fore'er in heaven in the LORD's house, dwell.

There are many different belief systems, and the final thing that I would note about mine is that its central figure, Jesus, placed a lot of emphasis on something that he called the "church". I spent a lot of time in church Sunday mornings, and Sunday and Wednesday evenings. I spent so much time in churches growing up that I developed a natural aversion to them now. Now I participate in the Chinese home church movement. I am blessed to be part of that community and other communities that are related to my beliefs. My community relates to the question of The Task about where I can best serve.

Because my belief system places such an emphasis on communities (churches), it has a special significance for the question of The Task, where can you serve? If you are wanting to dedicate yourself to your belief system, that may reflect that you have a desire for strong internal consistency. Internal logical consistency is a strong predictor of long-term economic growth, because that consistency can help you create systems. Systems can be implemented mindlessly to generate cash independently of your effort (businesses that you own, and that other people can work on). Systems can project you on a course of growth.

If you have a strong faith-based system, I encourage you to identify if there is a community that is affiliated with your faith. If so, that may be an excellent place to serve. Alternatively, it may not be. I recommend several other worthy charitable organizations in this book, including ones that Real Advisers directly supports.

As an alternative to an existing community, you could create your own. In Chapter 12 entitled "Your Focus", I describe how I and some friends formed a tax exempt, woman-led nonprofit corporation, Merciful Gardener Foundation Inc. The charitable purpose of MGF is to house and feed the poor on a sustainable basis. I serve on the three-person Board of Directors of MGF along with our President, Amanda Raby, and another of our friends, Caitlin Austin. (Amanda is a phenomenally talented vocal artist and magician and created covers for my Chalm poetry books.) This is a little community of people outside my belief system, but they certainly are informed of my belief system through the name of the corporation. In fact, our name pays homage to the story from Luke's Gospel about the parable of the merciful gardener. Chalm's version is here:

> The gardener who in the vineyard works,
> one day its owner asked him to explain:
> "The past three years, I come here seeking fruit.
> This fig tree from production still abstains.
>
> "Why should it waste the precious dirt this way?
> I'm now suggesting that you cut it down."
> Instead, proposing this alternative,
> the dresser of the vines described its ground:

"Sir, one more year, the soil around its roots.
Aeration, and manure I will apply.
If once again, no fruit appears next year,
I'll cut it down, throw it into the fire."

I love this parable (and poem) and the emphasis on the notion of the "merciful gardener". His seeking mercy for the unproductive fig tree gives me a message of eternal hope about the possibility of redemption for not only my life but for everyone's. No matter the many mistakes I made in my life, there is always the possibility for forgiveness.

Another way to say it is that there is always the possibility for overcoming the bad karma that you build up for yourself. You must take specific action, and frequently exercise great humility. In doing so, though, you will reveal to yourself the cognitive biases that impair your ability to trend in the direction of wealth accumulation. You also will be exercising the love that the universe has for you and that I believe it desires that we share with one another. I make the argument elsewhere that serving your community in humility is actually in your own best interests. I hope you become convinced of that as you read this book.

Chapter 5

The Task—Who Am I?

This is obviously a big question.

Plato's Apology describes Socrates' famous dictum: "The unexamined life is not worth living." You may have heard this saying before.

Self-knowledge may be a painful thing for you. There may be disappointments or trauma in your past that crushed your core identity. Because things happened to you in a way that was contrary to your vision (i.e., reasonable expectations for safety and respect), your identity may have been so bruised by the violence done to it that looking into your identity now is a painful exercise. When you look into your identity, all you may see is the wounded child or the woman who was a victim of a sexual assault. You see yourself as someone who has survived trauma but has not overcome it. That traumatized person lives inside you and seems to represent the core of your identity in the sense that the wounded portion is the most easily identifiable part. We are naturally inclined to pay attention to our wounds. We have an interest in binding up wounds and making sure they are not so severe that they kill us. When you are seriously wounded, that is all you can think about.

    The bad thing about the wounds from trauma is that they never seem to heal. You relive the trauma over and over even though the event that created the trauma occurred years ago. Events and people who remind you of the traumatic event trigger your emotional responses, so that you respond unreasonably to situations in the present. Your involuntary flight-or-flight response causes you to react to events and people (including people you love) in an inappropriate or unkind way. Unprocessed trauma interferes with our ability to establish close interpersonal relationships because it impairs our ability to have a healthy relationship with ourselves.

    If every time you look inside, you see a wounded child, you avoid having to look inside because that wounded child is you, and she appalls you. You remember the time before the trauma occurred and wish that you could return the child to that time. From thereon, you could proceed along a new timeline to now, so that instead when you look inside, the child you see (as yourself) will be happy and smiling. The child will have avoided the trauma and can now take full advantage of the opportunities she finds in her path in a way that is entirely consistent with her natural inclinations and curiosities.

Here is where meditation can help a lot. Many times, the wounded child can experience healing if you can simply sit with her in acceptance in silence. The acceptance is this, that the alternative timeline that I described above is impossible. We all know the people in our lives who wish they only could return to that earlier time when everything was perfect, or at least preferable to the way things are now. Time machines are impossible so acceptance means that we cannot go back. We only have the present and must find something that will allow the wounded child to move forward.

Meditation helped me to sit in silence with my unresolved anger toward my ex-wife, Aricka. I am moving forward past this anger and am taking active, specific steps to rid anger toward her from my heart completely. I still must discipline my thoughts. This requires constant attention and mindfulness. It is easy for me to re-engage with that anger and feed it and cause it to grow. My friends know this about me and help keep me from going to dark places in my conversations. I now focus on saying and thinking positive things about Aricka even though it is difficult sometimes.

I mention meditation and that serves as a practice that can help process trauma. It is helping me tremendously with my anger at my ex-wife associated with the trauma of my divorce that I held onto for a long time. For more severe trauma, I would highly recommend that you read the chapter on Trauma and Psychedelics now (Chapter 11) to learn about some exciting new natural treatment modalities (therapies) that are being used to treat post-traumatic stress disorder (PTSD) and other mental health issues. Psychedelic science is a hot topic right now in 2020 and Real Advisers intends to support research into psychedelics. We want to be involved directly with a clinic where our clients can take advantage of these healing PTSD therapies as well as therapies for mental health issues like addiction, depression, and anxiety, in a safe and legal environment. Because of the United States' antiquated and genuinely evil drug possession laws, our trauma clinic likely will be in Mexico. We are focusing on the Yucatan.

No matter what, meditation can be used to get in touch with the essential core of who you are as a person. I would recommend that if you have specific questions about meditation, go read Chapters 15 and 16 now so that you can begin to understand this key concept. The sooner that you can begin developing a consistent meditation practice, the sooner you will be on the road to becoming wealthier in a way that is consistent with the principles of this book.

What I would encourage you to start looking for in yourself when asking the question, who am I? are your highest attributes, the most noble things about you, the things about you that you like the most.

Is there nothing about yourself that you like? If the answer is "no," I can understand and relate to the feeling. I describe elsewhere in this book that in 2012 I thought my life was no longer worth living. I could find nothing in my life that I liked. I was divorcing, I was sad about my kids, I hated my job, and I wondered why I ever became an attorney. I was miserable, and that misery informed me that death was preferable to life. This was a lie, and I am so thankful that I did not succeed in my plans to kill myself. It would have wounded my kids and my parents in an extraordinary way, and I am ashamed that I got to a place where it seemed like my only option was suicide.

The pain of my existence was so great that I thought non-existence would alleviate that pain. It probably would have, but the undeniable fact is that my suicide would have caused an extraordinary amount of additional, lifelong pain for my loved ones who survived me. My kids would have lived the rest of their lives with the knowledge that their dad hated himself so much that he thought his only solution was suicide. Every time they thought that it would make them sad. Describing it would make me cry except I am at a place now when I am optimistic about the future and I have so much to live for. My kids are the main people in my life I try to serve, and I would do anything for them. This is not an uncommon feeling among parents, but I have not always been able to connect with that feeling as strongly as I do now.

I wish that I had an easy answer for people who are suicidal. The intrusive ideations can be so tempting in that they entice you into believing that the pain can end, and the lie that everyone left behind will be better off. In fact, you start to think that they may be happier now that you are gone. They may be relieved that the problem Roland is gone and finally they can begin to live their lives in enjoyment, free of his presence. This is a lie.

The reason I know this is a lie has to do with a core belief underlying The Offer. This core belief is that the universe, or God, created you. You didn't ask to be born, did you? Your existence must be said to be involuntary unless you remember in your past lives that something you did then somehow propelled you here. I am open to other understandings of identity and discussions about where we presently sit on the eternal timelines of our existence. For most of us, though, we identify with a notion that our identity began at a specific point in time, our birth. I don't want to be disrespectful to past-lives or reincarnation believing people. Don't get me wrong.

I've made an argument here that your existence proves that you have a purpose. Logically, this is known as an invalid tautology *unless* you accept the premise of an underlying benevolent universe that has specific awareness of your presence and included you in its design. With that in mind, think about your beliefs. I accept that everyone has their own belief system.

Maybe the arguments I am making here will be hardest for people who view the universe as mechanistic and absent of any special "awareness" or "consciousness". If you believe that the universe truly is a soulless system devoid of any intent, I recommend that you try psychedelics. A common experience among people who take psychedelics is a new feeling of interconnectedness to the universe. That accurately describes my experience.

In 2012, when I first took psilocybin-containing mushrooms in my successful (but desperate) attempt to heal my depression and stop my suicidal ideations, I had the sense of what it was like to be David when he describes in the Psalms that the LORD delighted in him. What a magnificent feeling to have the sense that the universe is aware of you and looks at you as its perfect creation without defect. Your existence is its own justification and your calling is to enjoy life. With the calling of love, we are invited to a life of service as well, but service that ultimately will serve your own best interests.

I mentioned above that if you hate yourself or find the self that is inside you revolting, you will have a hard time answering the question, who am I? Self-acceptance is extremely important to the notion of rest, because in order to rest, you must be at peace. If you don't accept yourself, you will never be at peace, and this will interfere with your industriousness, a precursor (usually) for wealth accumulation.

We've heard the saying that you can't love

anybody else until you first love yourself. I hated myself in 2012 when I was suicidal. I was unlovable and incapable of giving much love to anyone, even my kids. Since then, I have had to accept many uncomfortable truths about myself. I also have had some wonderful experiences, and I have recognized how tremendously gifted I have been by my universe. And according to my belief system, for that internal consistency, I remember that "to whom much is given, much is required." We are called to lives of service. I believe that the "much" required of me will come to fruition through Real Advisers and The Offer. I have had to let go of things in the past and move forward into this exciting new endeavor.

  What psychedelics and meditation brought to me was the 17-year-old Roland that I left behind so long ago. I told him that there was too much risk, and he was insufficient to the task, of becoming a creative writer. I traumatized myself with that message, and while I helped myself by telling myself to go to law school (where I in fact learned a lot about how to write), it was still trauma. Reconnecting with that 17-year-old wannabe Kurt Vonnegut has made all the difference in my life since 2012.

Two Ayahuasca ceremonies in 2015 propelled me on a path of writing creatively and on a regular basis for the first time in my life. I was 44. This path led me to write my "T. H. Chalm" poetry that almost exclusively has been focused on the five poetry books of the Bible and the Gospel of Matthew. I also wrote Les Club Des Hashischins: An Expressive Transliteration, a chapbook length poem re-telling Theophile Gautier's account of a cannabis club from the 1840s in Paris. I wanted to both glorify my God in my poetry but also glorify the part of his creation expressed in sacred healing plants. I didn't know how that would ever help me, but I loved it since I finally was making things that possibly could rescue the lonely 10-year-old boy whose best friends were books. As I describe elsewhere in this book, that lonely boy was (and still is) me.

When I received The Offer, I realized instantaneously that it incorporated every area of interest in my life. I will continue to use my legal skills professionally as a working attorney representing corporate and securities law clients, but I also want to spend as much of my creative energy as possible helping QuetzalHiloco and Real Advisers develop the concepts I describe in The Offer.

In part, The Offer is a gamifiable lead generation and team building tool for Real Advisers. It is based on universal principles described in this book with which everyone (maybe) can identify. Remember, Real Advisers is a heart-centered financial advisory firm that seeks to help you get in touch with defining wealth and how to achieve it for yourself. To truly implement successful strategies for clients, though, Real Advisers is going to be up front about meditation and the use of psychedelics to heal trauma. In this book, I share with you accounts of how I am healing my own trauma. The hopeful thing for you about this is that my experiences are not unusual and can be replicated. I am not the ultimate guide for what I describe in this book, but I include references to those ultimate guides.

Much of this book is about overcoming personal trauma, whether from violence, abuse, death, or divorce, because everyone experiences trauma to some degree during their lives. Everyone can recognize the debilitating effects of trauma and traumatic experiences. While trauma is inevitable and unavoidable, what we do with the trauma that happens to us is what matters. I discuss trauma in The Offer because unprocessed trauma is a drag on wealth accumulation.

The Offer is the answer to The Task for Roland Wiederaenders. I intend to tell you who I think I am, what I think I want, and how I think I can best serve, in the chapters of this book. If I am off base in any of what I describe, I'm writing this in part as an open letter to some people who know me well and have for a long time, including my parents. I would appreciate their insights.

One final thought about the "Who am I?" question. I make this note in the following chapter, that sometimes it may be harder for you to think about your identity than it is for you to think about your wants. I wanted to let you know that you don't have to answer the questions of The Task in order. I answered my questions by starting with what I wanted right after my divorce. As a heterosexual man who had just lost the only sexual partner he ever had, what do you think I wanted when after 16 years I was no longer married?

My poetry started in earnest in 2014 when I wrote several love poems to a woman I highly admired (and still do), Sarah "Agent Red" Johnston. While she did not reciprocate my romantic feelings, she asked to use one of my poems, "One Word," in a dance and theatrical production named *Twist* that she staged in Austin. Red is a recognized artist and her encouragement and use of one of my poems in this public way gave me motivation to keep writing. That Red thought so highly of my poetry made me believe that it had merit and that I should continue to write. As I describe elsewhere, I later changed the erotic themes of my poetry to Biblical, but without Red's encouragement in this way, I may never have continued writing creatively. I owe Red so much for her artistic inspiration and she has been a great friend to me.

Chapter 6

The Task—What Do You Want?

We think that you will be able to walk away from accepting The Offer (which earns you the money it takes to perform five hours of work at your best ever hourly rate) with a task (The Task) to perform that will serve your financial best interests. When we make The Offer to you, we immediately pay you The Offer Price. You can perform the services while you are showering or driving. After performing The Task and understanding The Bible Study, you should have sufficient knowledge and information necessary to help yourself or anybody else in your life who has wealth but can't seem to enjoy it, or, someone you love who is super talented but just can't seem to make ends meet. That person would benefit from the thought exercise incorporated in The Task by attempting to specifically identify why they are unhappy. If their basic needs are met, they are unhappy because their wants are not being met. What is it that they want and how can they get it?

The question about your wants should be answered truthfully and honestly.

It may be easier for people to identify with what they want than who they are. This is the case because so many of us have experienced trauma or abuse where our core identities, and even our physical bodies, were invaded by outside trauma. I discuss trauma and its drag on wealth accumulation throughout this book. The result of trauma literally is to cause damage to your identity. That identity must be repaired before you can really begin to answer the question of who you are. Helping heal trauma through new natural modalities is a central focus of Real Advisers.

Our wants are frequently associated with our natural desires and human needs. I get hungry and would rather eat steak than beans and rice. On my diet now, I only may eat the steak (and other meat) as I am a strict carnivore. I discuss this diet and the keto diet in Chapter 18 entitled "Diet and Wellness". I both need food but want the specific food that works best for my body, so I prefer one over the other. Since I want meat that is more expensive than beans and rice, I need to make sure that I have sufficient income to pay for my extravagant lifestyle choice. Because the cost difference between meat and beans and rice, while significant, can be managed through budgeting, I decide to make this expenditure a priority. I make this decision because I know that my purchase of steak (and hamburger) actually is trending me in the direction of long-term wealth accumulation. That is the case because the meat not only brings me nutrition, but also, because my wants are being met too, it brings me rest. I could survive on rice and beans if I had to, but the meat satisfies me better. I find that my athletic performance is vastly more improved at 49 than ever before since I've made the dietary changes I describe here and later in this book. My point of this paragraph is that we can have wants that are associated with our needs.

We also can have wants that are not associated with our needs. I didn't need to rip out the ugly green carpet of the house I just moved into and replace it with stained concrete floors and hand knotted rugs. I could have left the old, stained carpet in. I would not have died from the rug like I would have died eventually if I didn't eat the rice and beans. I decided that my design with the concrete and throw rugs would give me enough rest that the additional expense was justified. This is how we justify any luxury purchase even if it means you are going to shop at The Gap instead of Old Navy. At one time in my life that represented my indulgence of a desire for luxury.

What do you want to do when you stop working?

Do you imagine a life of ease on the golf course and going home for an evening of drinking? Do you imagine serving as a volunteer with a tax-exempt organization you created 10 years ago that supports your grandchildren's school or sports league? It has grown so large based on your initial $25,000 contribution that now you can sit back and simply volunteer. You are enjoying an opportunity to serve your grandchildren in an organization that you helped create, and in the process, you reduced your federal income tax burden. Which of those options sounds better to you?

If you like to golf, great! Did you see I said sports league? Create a golf team booster club and make sure you are taking your grandkids golfing with you. Invest in a company like Golfinity Inc. in Austin that is using simulator technology to bring a Top Golf experience to the strip mall. Take your grandkids there throughout the week and bring their entire team along to support the business.

What do you want? Do you want to be on a boat in your retirement? Make sure you are finding a place to live where there is a body of water nearby and maybe you can take steps to learn about boating now, taking classes or volunteering as a deck hand. People are not specific enough in the articulation of their wants based on my own personal experience. They also do not take advantage of immediately available opportunities to pursue their desires as a result of lack of information and/or imagination.

People have a great capacity for self-deception regarding their desires. I have experienced this in my life. When I was 17, I told myself that I wanted to be a creative writer. I was a rabid Lord of the Rings fan and I loved The Hobbit too of course. I devoured science fiction, Dune, Asimov, William Gibson, and so much other fantasy literature and fiction. I loved to read and growing up in an isolated location without other kids nearby (in the days before the internet), books were a great source of solace as a child. I loved to read and imagined my highest aspiration was to be a creative writer.

Two "truths" I thought I knew, though, was that I did not have sufficient life experience to be a creative writer then (untrue), and also, that there was so much risk involved, *I would never be successful* (only possibly true). I also fundamentally didn't believe in a universe that took into account not only my needs but also my wants.

When I talk about expectations in this book, if they are necessities (like personal safety), they are wants. They are a part of our natural inclinations and curiosities influenced by aptitudes, all of which are universe-created. Another way of saying this is that your attributes are "God-given". Our exercise of wants is our exercise of the divine power that lives inside of us. Our agency is our capacity to take action in a godlike way.

In my tradition, I would say that Jesus lives inside of me, that I have been crucified with Christ, and I am a new creature. This means that my existence has been purified in the sense that, after my death, I am convinced of an eternal resurrection with continuity of my identity into a new material existence in a new heavens and a new earth.

I also believe that I am a godlike being now, also in the sense that with Jesus (the divine) inside me, frequently I feel like his love is flowing through me to other people whom, if I were left to my own devices, I would not love. I also find peace in the notion of the eternal durability of my existence. I get less hung up on things by focusing on the Buddhist truth that everything is temporary.

Maybe you believe in karma where you are able to

accumulate karma on this side in the hopes of a better reincarnation. Here again, our beliefs are so co-incident that distinctions would lead us to unnecessary arguments at a time while there are still hungry and homeless people in the world. I'm good with calling our good intentions karma as long as the poor are being served. If we don't manifest goodness, who will? Thank you Russell Brand.

    What this all regards is our magical ability to effect change in our universe. We all have the magical ability to manifest our desires into existence, but many people have a hard time identifying with this.

    If you feel powerless now, please understand that I felt that way as well when I erupted at a co-worker (whom I will refer to as Lorie). I had been so traumatized by my divorce that the mere fact that Lorie reminded me of my ex-wife caused me to be triggered. As a result of a triggering one day, I sent a co-worker an unkind and unprofessional email. I tell you more about this event in Chapter 15 because it was this event that brought me to meditation.

    After my email, I resigned from my position at the company in shame. I had told myself the lie that I had resolved my anger, but I regularly engaged in feeding that anger, increasing it and cultivating it like a garden. I was drinking poison and hoping Aricka would die from it. I was so powerless to my anger that I damaged a valuable interpersonal relationship to my economic detriment. I lost out on a valuable opportunity, but I learned a lesson from that failure: unprocessed trauma is a detractor from the long-term accumulation of wealth.

What is strong predictor of the creation of long-term wealth accumulation is clear thinking and clear action unimpeded by trauma. Clear thinking and clear action are implementing and directing your expectations and wants. Those expectations and desires are expressions of the divine inside you. The universe will enable those wants if your wants are aligned with it, and they can be. When you are exercising your divine power, you are a god. You are creating and bringing about a new existence that never has been before. You have aligned with the universe, and specifically sought to align your will, as much as is within your specific control and as much as you can perceive it with your limited perception, with what the universe wills. You remain open to any deviations or indications that either your will and wants, or your perception of the universe's will, is out of alignment. You recalibrate as best you can and continue.

My will was out of the will of the universe when I erupted at my co-worker, Lorie. I know this is the case because the fundamental principle of the universe is love, and I violated the love that I am ordered to by the being that I identify as "god". My God, Jesus, commanded me to love my brother (and sister) like myself. When I was unkind to Lorie, I directly contradicted my God's command. My will was not aligned with that of the universe. One way of saying it is that I sinned. Another way of describing my failure is to say that I accumulated some bad karma. I later attempted to remedy it by apologizing to Lorie.

Despite my apology, my unkind response to Lorie certainly hurt her. It was a violation of her expectations to be treated as a normal human being with respect. She, like all of us, held a perception of universal justice. This sense caused Lorie to have the reasonable and ordinary expectation that she would not be abused by her co-worker. Our perception of that universal justice is accurate, and in fact, underlying our expectation is not only a perception of justice, but of a mercy transcending justice. I believe that that the universe says to everyone that no matter what has happened in the past, there is a path for redemption. You can overcome any past obstacles, reattach to your identity, and begin expressing your will, your wants, and live and inhabit your full identity in a safe place. The universe wants to enable that.

If you do not identify with this, I understand. I was powerless when I erupted at Lorie. I had been cobbled by my anger. Then immediately after that event our partner Saurabh asked me about meditation. Meditation has changed my life, because now when I feel powerless, I have a tool and a place to go to that gives me a powerful sense of agency. I can direct my thoughts and identify that I am one of the central players of the game of the universe, just as you are. I can get this sense even at those moments when my wants are being stymied.

Meditation is a tool that you can use to look within yourself. I would encourage you to seek out the divine within yourself, not in an egotistical way but humbly because you represent an expression of the universe's intention. If you were not intended to exist, you wouldn't. That is only tautology if you say that there is no intent behind the universe. I understand that you may believe that the universe is more like a machine then a grandfatherly white dude with a white beard, robes and glowing halo. This may be one of those limitations that disqualify you from The Offer. This is the case only if you do not believe in your unlimited divine potential, because this is a fundamentally self-limiting belief. I know how self-limiting this belief can be from observations of my own life and how I have perceived myself inaccurately in the past.

    My dad and I had a unique conversation about his responses to The Task and what he wanted. One of the reasons that I am so convinced that The Offer will be successful is because during the course of writing this book, I was led to call my dad and invite him to participate in The Bible Study after about a year and a half of not talking.

    My relationship with my dad has been strained throughout my life. We have had extended periods where I have been unable to talk to him because of what I perceived as emotional abuse. Nevertheless, as a grown man I want to continue to interact with my dad, because I understand that any abuse that he may have inflicted on me was the result of abuse that he experienced himself. The unprocessed trauma in his life affected mine, but my dad did not have the same opportunities for healing that I have had.

My point is that when my dad and I were talking about his responses to The Task, he told me that his ideal living arrangement will always include a garden. He loves gardening and nature and would be miserable in an apartment in the middle of the city where he couldn't get outside every day and tend to some growing plants surrounding the place where he lived. An apartment in the middle of the city is in fact my ideal, so I told him, "Dad, if you ever live with me, if I really want to serve you, I should have a house where you can get outside and garden." He laughed.

I note that this story about my dad illustrates the principle of abundance, in that even though "they" are not making any more real estate, there is more than enough to go around. This is the case because I am happy in an apartment in a (luxury) multi-family property, but everyone has their own notion of an ideal living space. I have better clarity about what my dad wants simply by dialoguing with him about The Task and staying present enough with him by limiting our conversation to The Bible Study and The Task. I was able to hear his logician's mind express his knowledge and interpretation of Ecclesiastes and reveal more to me about himself in a way that I didn't hear before. (I describe my dad's advanced educational background in the next chapter.) This was all enabled by my ability to stay present with uncomfortable thoughts. I went to my meditation mantra multiple times in that conversation, but despite the stress, our talk yielded some powerful illustrations for this book.

I'll share with you what I really want. I want Real Advisers to find a brilliant, heart-centered wealth adviser who is senior to me, who meditates, and who believes in the words of The Offer. There is a better person than me to take Real Advisers to the next steps. I will work with Real Advisers as long as my Board needs me, but I also am informing them in this chapter about MY wants. The Offer came to me when I realized that what I really want to do is go back to school as a full-time student to get a Master of Fine Arts in poetry. I want to improve my poetry in the hopes that it might gain recognition from people who think a lot about poetry from an academic perspective. Maybe they can help me make it more relatable too. As an evangelist of what I perceive as the good news of my religion, I want to connect with people and be a witness to them about the awesome universe that I perceive. There are people out there who need encouragement. I frequently think that improving my writing may be the best way for me to serve.

Don't forget my prayer, though, that AS ABOVE, SO BELOW. I have imperfect understanding of heaven's intentions, so I am asking my Board of Advisors (my community) to advise me about my perceptions and tell me the answer to the question about how I can best serve. I'm a little suspect of my MFA ambition honestly because of how much it has to do with my pride. Remember, I said I wanted recognition from those professors? I may have a cognitive bias here and if I explore my motivations, I may see that my desire for an MFA may not be consistent with who I am or how I can best serve. I'm asking my closest friends and business partners to help me answer the questions of The Task for myself.

The following chapter describes another calling from my source text. My source text advocates that we should live lives full of love and service. Have you ever heard "love your brother like yourself"? This leads us to the question about how you can serve.

Chapter 7

The Task—How Can I Best Serve?

Throughout my life, I would grow nervous when I thought about the notion of service because of the economic circumstances in which I grew up.

I grew up in not exactly a poor household (I never lacked food, clothes, or shelter), but I heard "no" a lot from my mom when I asked for things I wanted that cost money. To help me alleviate my boredom, she knew I was smart and directed me to things that did not cost money (books from the library) to my great blessing.

My dad also encouraged me to read. Reading and writing are essential for him as he is highly intelligent, and he holds a post-graduate degree in theology (a Master of Divinity) that required extensive study of multiple ancient languages like Hebrew, Latin, and Greek. My love of books, reading, and writing, influenced strongly by both parents, has blessed my adult life greatly. In law, I found a personally rewarding career, and my creative writing gives me the deepest sense of personal meaning.

Because I grew up in humble economic circumstances, I focused a lot on money in my younger adult life when I thought about my professional career.

Consequently, the risk of becoming a professional creative writer seemingly contradicted my desire for money. When I told myself the lies at 17 about being a creative writer, I did tell myself something wise and precocious, and something that I know was inspired by my source because of the way my life played out. I told myself, "too much risk being a creative writer, but go to law school and learn how to write there in a profession where you can be paid much more to write than in any other profession." This was only partially true for another reason because I didn't know at the time that a hedge fund manager could combine both words AND numbers and make even more than J. K. Rowling or Alan Dershowitz.

My focus on money made me skeptical toward the notion of working for free which was all I could think of when I heard the word "service". I put my head down, got my undergraduate and law degrees as fast as I could, and for the first years of my career, focused on the highest paying job I could get, not caring whether it was something that I really wanted to do. Money was my central object.

Even though I was hyper-focused on money, I know the universe carried me along the path that it wanted me to go on. All during this time I kept saying that prayer, "not my will, Universe, but yours," and of course, the universe enabled its intention and directed me here. Now with my creative words and a few numbers that I am mostly going to leave to my partners, I can create not only great investment value and personal growth opportunities for people, but also satisfy the craving that I had as a 17-year-old to someday write books that millions of people might read and actually enjoy. This book will also work to your economic profit.

I remained skeptical of service, but one thing my source document instructed me to do is tithe. Tithing is a Biblical concept where you are supposed to give a tenth ($1/10^{th}$) of your gross income to the LORD. People here in the United States interpret that as giving money to the church specifically, the institution that owns the dirt where the building with the steeple sits. That is not the only way to "give unto the LORD".

For many years, I tithed regularly to the church I attended with my family. Simultaneously with my divorce from my ex-wife, Aricka, I also "divorced" the church we were attending. I expressed a lot of anger toward some men and women from the congregation there who had tried to help Aricka and I reconcile. In the process I sinned against them, or another kinder (but in my mind less accurate) way of describing this is that I built up a lot of bad karma for myself. Since that time, I went back to try to remedy my eruptions at the church members. Do you see a recurring theme in my life? My eruption at Lorie (described elsewhere in this book) and my eruption at the church elders were rooted in the same fundamental problem, my unresolved anger issues. I had a fundamental belief that neither my wants nor my needs would ever be satisfied, and this world would be nothing but toil and pain for me. I was triggered by unresolved childhood trauma and lashed out in desperation in situations when I was unable to regulate emotions.

    I did not believe that the universe loved me or had incorporated me into its design. In fact, I wrote in my journal in 2012 that my kids would be better off with the $2 million from my life insurance policy than with a living dad. This is insanity and mental illness, but yet, that was my mental state. I had recovered a lot by 2017 (2012 was both my bottom and when my dramatic upswing began to occur), but I still carried trauma from my divorce, this unresolved anger and resentment that I had been cultivating toward Aricka.

How does this relate to service? My unresolved childhood trauma led to mental illness that prevented me from loving and serving Aricka and our kids. Consequently, we got a divorce. This led to great heartache for me, and I know it created the same heartache, expressed in different ways, for Aricka and my kids. My unresolved trauma not only prevented me from engaging with my family, but it also prevented me from engaging with that community that was centered around my belief system, the church.

My inability to empathize and emotionally self-regulate caused me to believe that the church elders and others who tried to help Aricka and me reconcile were not trying to help, but in fact were out to "get" me. I was so deluded, I believed that they had a secret intent to harm me. I was in an extremely angry place in my mind, and my anger and disruptive behavior (I stormed out of a meeting room, violently turning over a chair and shouting as I left) fractured my relationship with my community, the church.

I went back to those guys who were in that church conference room nearly seven years later and asked for their forgiveness. I told them that they were dealing with a very difficult person (me) in very difficult circumstances and they were doing their best with limited resources. I apologized to them for my inappropriate and abusive expressions of anger toward them and asked them to forgive me. They did so graciously.

I bring this up to humiliate myself to you, and to show you how easy it is. This is the case because the human character trait of humility is essential for true intimacy with other people. Humility also is a trait that trends people in the direction of long-term wealth accumulation. To cultivate humility, you must be willing to identify cognitive biases associated with pride. I devote all of Chapter 17 to a description of humility.

After 2012, I decided that I was going to try to seek a different community that wasn't oriented around the church. The community that I went to was the Multidisciplinary Association for Psychedelic Studies, or "MAPS". MAPS is a highly-credible tax exempt charitable organization based in Santa Cruz, California working to fund medical research demonstrating the safe efficacy of psychedelics as healing modalities for mental health issues. In 2013, I began donating time and money to MAPS, trying my best to "tithe" to them and other similar organizations just like I had with the church in the past. I was letting go of my wealth and releasing control over money that could have been used to satisfy my wants.

I tell this to you not to brag or to make myself look like a good person, but to give you an example of how I was serving a community in a way that was in accordance with my wants. This is the case because while I wanted a bunch of material things that my tithes could have bought for me, I had a simultaneous desire to think about how I can best serve. I was so impressed by the healing power of psychedelics from my own experience (psilocybin and cannabis saved me from suicide) that I wanted to help bring that healing about for other people. For the first time, I could see directly how I could love my brother like I loved myself by giving money to a cause that could bring about true mental health healing. It seemed like medical research was a "nobler" cause even than the church itself because the medical research could bring about healing without requiring anyone to adopt an underlying belief system. I wanted to prevent my brothers and sisters who suffered from PTSD and depression from committing suicide and to experience the healing power of psychedelics just like I had. This was a healing power that was nothing like I had ever experienced, and this is common testimony from people whose mental illness has been alleviated by treatment with psychedelics. I believe that this is a somewhat of a desperate need, or at least urgent, because of the evil drug possession laws in the United States and throughout the world that have so adversely effected research into this area and accessibility of these natural plants, cactus, and mushroom.

Another thing that I talk about in the chapter on federal income tax planning is the principle that if you live in the United States, you must violate the Income Tax Code of 1986, as amended (the "Code", the governing statute for the Internal Revenue Service (IRS) and all the Treasury Department Regulations) to keep 100% of the money you earn from your job. There are laws about paying yourself a reasonable salary even if you run your own business. While you can do many things to manage taxes on your unearned income, if you are working at a job and being paid on a W2 (even if from your own business), you must withhold the self-employment, Medicare, and Social Security taxes and pay those to the IRS at least quarterly. This does not include any obligations that you have at the state level, but the same principles apply.

You can plan to reduce your tax burden on unearned income. Unearned income (profits from your business) is not associated with a corresponding employment tax withholding obligation. If you do not effectively manage your unearned income, you will pay federal income tax on that amount.

You have no choice but to pay the employment taxes, but you do have the choice to pay the income tax on unearned income. This is the case because the tax Code allows you to deduct the costs of certain expenditures against income (subject to certain limitations). For purposes of this chapter, every dollar that you donate to any qualified tax-exempt charitable organization described under Section 501(c)(3) of the Code can be deductible against your income (subject to certain AGI limitations). These organizations could provide jobs and serve benevolent purposes like a church does. Alternatively, a Section 501(c)(3) entity could be like our Merciful Gardener Foundation Inc., a charitable, low-income housing tax exempt nonprofit corporation. Our purpose is to house and feed the poor. Through donations to tax-exempt organizations, you can choose to direct your charitable giving to a nonprofit that you potentially could exercise a great deal of influence and control over as one of its founding board members. You are creating a community of people that you can serve in a way that you can control and influence. If you don't want to mop, then include a budget to hire a cleaning crew and create jobs in the process. My point of this is that there are many different ways to serve and you are going to be in a position of authority if you are the chief donor and/or a board member of a tax-exempt non-profit corporation that you helped found.

People don't understand that if they resent having to pay federal income taxes, it can be optional to do so. Please talk to our tax planners about this matter, but the truth is that you may not have to pay any income tax to the IRS. The only thing that you must do is decide to give money to charitable organizations and engage in certain other tax planning. There is no rule that says that you cannot donate to an organization that you helped found or that you help manage.

Through my support of MAPS, I wanted to support the science behind what I knew to be true, the healing power of psychedelics (psilocybin and cannabis in my case) applied to mental health maladies, depression and anxiety, that I had struggled with for a long time. I knew of the research that MAPS conducted and so I gave money to them. This connected me to a small community in Austin and throughout the United States of other people who also were MAPS supporters.

Through this community I have met some of the most interesting, compassionate, and dedicated people in the world. Most of the scientists studying psychedelics through MAPS and other similar organizations do so purely for the love of the science and the help that they believe they are bringing about, but not for financial gain. Many of the MAPS supporters are artists and other entrepreneurs who identify with the emphasis on expression that the Burning Man culture promotes. I strongly identify with expression as a calling on my life because love never speaks without a voice.

The founder of MAPS, Rick Doblin, is a personal hero. Rick followed the same path to wealth that I describe in this book. Rick Doblin (at least as I perceive him) is a wealthy man no matter his bank account (of which I have no specific knowledge). I say this because Rick is totally engaged with who he is: he identifies through his Jewish faith that he has a calling to take steps to prevent another Holocaust from ever happening again. MAPS is strongly connected to Rick's identity. He also is connected to what he wants. For a LONG time, Rick has had the goal of creating an organization that is working to legalize therapeutic psychedelics. He also serves, as Rick believes that MAPS will help alleviate mental illness through its research. Rick has been successful in his goal (with the help of many others) as now in 2020 MAPS has nearly obtained FDA approval for MDMA as a safe and effective treatment for PTSD.

One cannot help but be impressed by the evident science in this area that shows that this new MDMA therapy has potential in a way that NOTHING ever has had before. The results are so positive that the scientists don't believe their own data. The results of successful treatment of PTSD with MDMA are repaired lives and relationships because people are able to overcome debilitating trauma that has been interfering with their ability to conduct business, earn an income, and maintain interpersonal relationships. Debilitating trauma is a strong detractor from the ability to accumulate long-term heart-centered wealth.

Rick Doblin is a wealthy man by The Offer's measure for sure and illustrates the notion of service perfectly.

You may be called on to render actual volunteer

services that do in fact take away from time you could otherwise use to earn an income. Before missing your supposed lost income too soon, consider a book like Give and Take by Adam Grant that presents strong empirical evidence that givers, whether of time or money, are more likely than not to make more money and achieve greater lifetime wealth (measured by actual dollars) than non-givers.

He gives many reasons for this, and one of the main ones is that givers, people who contribute to communities and who put more in than they take out, are looked upon favorably by their communities. This is self-evident. When I pay you The Offer Price for The Task you are going to look favorably on me as someone who just gave you free money. The community I represent is Real Advisers and I hope that you look so favorably on our community that you decide to hire us as your wealth advisors.

The people in the communities that look favorably on the givers proceed along in their normal day to day lives. Then one day, a hailstorm occurs, and the Millers need a new roof. For their roof replacement, they pick the roofer they know from church, Robert, the guy they always see volunteering and contributing there in different ways. Because the Millers (a husband and wife) are on the church's finance committee, they know confidentially that this blue-collar roofer who "only" graduated from high school gives over $20,000 to his church EVERY YEAR because his roofing business is so successful. They don't pick the random roofer from the phone book because they don't know him. The unknown roofer may do a terrific job, and maybe even do the work more cheaply than their friend from church. The Millers almost do not even care because they know their friend gives back to his community.

What the Millers know is that when they pay Robert, a significant portion of what they pay him will be paid back to their community through his annual giving in a way that is going to benefit everyone. They live by the positivist proposition that all boats rise in the tide and they also believe in abundance. When I call the Millers for a recommendation of a roofer, who will they recommend? Do you think Robert's business is blessed by the universe?

There is also the notion from my source text that "to whom much is given, much is required." The universe did not give you your natural inclinations, curiosities, resources, talents, wants, and desires *solely* for our own benefit and enjoyment, though it certainly did give those to you for that reason. It also gave you those gifts so that you could perform our essential calling that I referenced above, the calling to love. We are called to love one another and that means service. If you are not living in the fullness of your identity as a creature called to service, you never will enjoy any amount of wealth because you will be isolated and separate from any community that could give back to you and encourage you.

Your community can give you the feeling of fulfillment that comes when you are loved, and the desire for love should be everyone's want. I believe that was how we were created. Love is the answer to the question about how you enjoy wealth, and it is the same answer whether you are rich and poor, since no matter how much money you have, you can always love and receive love. When you experience that love, you will feel peace and contentment, and that unmistakably is the state of the enjoyment of wealth that Solomon wrote about in Ecclesiastes as being "blessed".

This reveals an essential message and characteristic of The Offer. The Offer is made to everyone. The universe has made The Offer to you to perform The Task. For you to make The Wager with the universe, just invest every dollar you own in yourself and your natural inclinations. Join me in telling the universe that you want to serve, but confess that service scares you because you are afraid that if you aren't selfish, your needs will go unmet. Tell the universe that you believe it enables its intentions, and that in fact you are the focus of its intentions. It has specific awareness of you and it loves you with an indescribable love that you can do nothing to increase or decrease. Tell the universe that you want to align your will with it (AS ABOVE, SO BELOW), and be honest even, informing the universe of the practicality of your decision, that you have elected not to challenge it, but to flow with it. That is a thing.

The universe will respond to help you create infinite wealth. You will make The Offer to Bill Gates on its ordinary terms and say to him, "Someday, Bill, if you work hard, your rate will be like mine, infinite." I'm using him as an easy target. If you are reading this, Bill, I'm sure you can see the hyperbole and exaggeration for humorous effect. The underlying idea of The Offer (your personal infinite value, proved by your existence) reinforces this notion, and you plausibly agree with all the principles described here. About 99.9% of the people who read this can.

Bill Gates doesn't have the problem of the demoralized person who can't perceive his own self-worth. Every person on the planet (including Bill himself) recognizes the near infinite value that the universe enabled him to create if they have ever happened to turn on a computer. Bill envisioned a future with a new reality, DOS and Windows, and brought that reality about by employing the character traits described herein as generally trending people in the direction of long-term wealth accumulation.

Whether Bill Gates enjoys his wealth is a question that would need to be answered by his intimates. If the concepts in this book (based on the ancient wisdom of Solomon) are true, then I believe that Bills Gates truly is wealthy. The reason I believe this is because Bill Gates is focused on service. Wikipedia informed me that by 2018, Bill and Melinda Gates had donated $36 billion to a charitable Section 501(c)(3) tax-exempt foundation that they appropriately named "Bill & Melinda Gates Foundation". That is a lot of money by any measure.

Bill answered the question, how can I best serve?

by donating a large portion of his own personal net worth to a charitable organization. Of course, his donations are tax deductible (subject to limitations) so he is saving on taxes and he gets a lot of good press from the foundation. This is an organization that he has enormous influence over for sure but also one that employs 1,602 people. His foundation has made total grant payments since inception (through Q4 2019) of $54.8 billion. I am sad that Bill has gotten so much bad press due to Coronavirus/COVID-19. I do not personally believe he wants to chip you with his vaccine, but of course, I could be proved wrong completely. Why would that be true, though? He and all the other technology and cell phone companies already have chipped us with the cell phones we all carry in our pockets and purses. I believe that when Bill was writing those checks to the foundation he and his wife founded, it was an example of the same prayer that I pray, "Universe, I have a will of course, but when I think about my exercise of that will, please direct me according to what you intend. Practically, I would be a fool to try to contradict you, so I am trying to get on board with your program, with your agenda. Show me how I can serve." AS ABOVE, SO BELOW.

I have one final thought to share about the notion of service. We have incorporated a specific organizational element into Real Advisers' design so that it is a woman-led organization. The way that we have done this is to create an independent Board of Advisors that by charter provides for majority women control. Because we take people at their face value (or at least we try to), there is not going to be a specific inquiry into the gender composition of the Board, and the Board will be responsible for determining who its members should be.

I personally want to try to see people with God's eyes of love that influence me to believe that no one should be loved any differently or any less than everyone else. Particularly, we should love and serve people even if they are different from us, and even if there are aspects of their identities or personalities that we do not understand or maybe through our ignorance find offensive. Real Advisers is a completely inclusive organization.

Further, we will neither support nor serve anyone who promotes hatred and injustice. There are hungry people in the world that do not have a place to live, so we simply don't have time or energy to waste on hatred and injustice. Hatred and injustice are unacceptable to Real

Advisers.

The reason for Real Advisers' woman-led initiative is because we always want to be a heart-centered wealth management firm. There of course exist many heartless women, and there are many incredibly compassionate men. Because gender-based inequality continues to exist, to combat against that, I want to take direction from a group of people (a majority of whom are women) whom I believe are more likely than not to consider matters from the perspective of disenfranchised groups. Women have a capacity to identify with the disenfranchised because women so frequently still experience (at least a degree of) powerlessness in our society because of systemic gender discrimination. If I can attempt to remedy this by having a woman-led board, then that is what I will do.

While we arguably are at an all-time high for gender egalitarianism in the world, there remains work to be done. For us to best serve clients who focus on personal wealth creation for themselves and their communities, I believe Real Advisers will be best served by a women-led Board. This decision will be left up to the Board, but there will be a clear statement that all things being equal, this should be the Board composition.

Finally, I do not intend to serve on the Board, acknowledging that my true calling maybe lies elsewhere. I see myself as a replaceable cog in the Real Advisers world, and provided I am adequately compensated for my services and value for creating The Offer, I welcome the day that Real Advisers might ask me to step back from the initial leadership role I assume I will fill. I hold all attachments to our organizational structure loosely since we are in the process of forming our Board now.

Chapter 8

The Task—Your Hourly Rate

An essential component to The Task is your calculation and rationalization of your hourly rate. This is an important concept to any service provider. Whether you are a contractor of full-time employee, or working for yourself in your own business, you can always calculate your hourly rate.

Let's say that you never worked in your life, graduated from high school, and immediately went to work as a plumber's apprentice. Those were the only services that you ever performed, and you never worked anywhere else. To determine your hourly rate, just take whatever your salary is (or actual hourly rate) and divide by the number of hours you work. Don't include travel time because we want your rate to be as high as possible! If the plumber apprentice were paid $35,000 per year, then his hourly rate would be roughly $17.50 per hour if he worked 2,000 hours per year.

Let's name the plumber Mario. Let's say that one time in high school Mario had a friend who hired him to be a DJ. Mario had control of the sound system, and did an OK job playing songs that everyone liked at his friend's house party. At the end, Mario's friend gave him $50 for two hours of work. That was the best hourly rate that Mario ever got, and the party was right next to his house. There wasn't even any travel time to consider. In this case, for the purpose of The Task, I want Mario to say that his rate is $25 per hour (instead of $17.50), and I would pay him $125 dollars unconditionally just to perform The Task for himself. I would give him my feedback for free.

The $25 per hour represents his true potential, right? The one thing that Mario should do is remember that this is his potential, and if he wants more money and more time like most people, all things being equal, maximizing his hourly rate is in his best interests. Does this mean he should quit plumbing and be a full time DJ? Before making that decision, I would counsel Mario to carefully count the costs and make sure that he will work a sufficient number of hours per year in his new career as a DJ.

As I have discussed this with my friends, they understandably and inevitably make jokes about the world's oldest profession. (Both prostitutes and attorneys frequently bill by the hour. For this and other reasons, I have always thought the two professions were similar.) Even there, the hourly rate achieved at what may otherwise be a demeaning and demoralizing profession might be that person's current highest economic potential, if not the highest representation of themselves as a human being or what they could achieve financially. Getting that rate maybe carry with it a high personal cost or maybe not. As the news informs us, the illegal prostitution industry is dangerous, filled with violence, exploitation, and child trafficking. The personal cost to working in that industry must be high, but possibly it can be mitigated in countries where morals and laws allow prostitution to be a profession that can be conducted legally and out in the open.

Without wanting to dwell on this too much, what I find typically when I talk with people about their hourly rate is that I can imagine what they do, their interests, and their skill set, and how those could be applied in different ways. I almost always think that their hourly rate should be higher than what they think it is initially. I want to encourage people to see their highest potential.

Let's be clear that I would never encourage someone to prostitution but bring that example up to note that The Offer can apply to everyone. Maybe in jurisdictions where prostitution is not criminalized, we will have a Real Advisers representative who calls himself or herself the financial advisor to prostitutes. I am open to all possibilities.

Chapter 9
The Wager—Part 1

The way I make money starts with The Wager. When I have all your data and answers to the questions of The Task, you may want to know what I think of everything you just told me. After all, I paid you The Offer Price and I am holding myself out as an investment adviser who has knowledge that can help you grow your wealth.

One way of expressing The Wager is this: if your hourly rate is lower than mine, if you want to know what I think on a professional basis, you must agree to pay me for five hours of my time at my rate. That is The Wager.

If a person makes The Wager, this is the first piece of financial advice that I am going to tell them: when you go to most financial advisory firms, they are going to steer you toward products that are designed to compensate them in very specific ways. These financial products (think mutual funds, exchange traded funds (ETFs), bond funds) are focused almost exclusively on the public securities markets (Wall Street). What financial advisers are unlikely to discuss with you is how you can build wealth through real estate. The reason most wealth advisors do not discuss real estate is because it is more difficult, if not impossible, for them to be paid on real estate that you might invest in. The money that you invest in real estate is invested in a financial product (an asset) that does not generate income (commissions) for them.

With real estate, though, you can get safe, leveraged returns while satisfying a fundamental need that everyone has: the need to lay their head down on a pillow every night. We will tell you how to simultaneously meet this need of yours while achieving leveraged returns and building wealth in the process.

Real Advisers is an investment advisory firm focused on clients who want to invest a greater than average portion of their portfolio in real estate because they understand the power of leveraged returns. Our clients understand how powerful leveraged returns can be, but how risky margin can be in connection with trading in securities. We will talk about many other things during our five hours, but real estate will be the central focus of our conversation with respect to investment matters.

I discuss leveraged returns in Chapter 24 entitled "Real Estate and Leveraged Returns".

One element of The Wager is the hourly rate. My hourly rate with Real Advisers is $1,000 and when you make The Wager, you must agree to pay me five times that amount, $5,000! I know that sounds high. The way that it is paid can be accomplished in different ways, and if you are my friend, of course, I can give you my five hours for free.

Remember, one of the reasons that Real Advisers representatives are paid differently is because we are advising you about real estate in ways that traditional financial advisors either cannot or will not. We have less of an opportunity to make the traditional fees that financial advisers earn because we are steering you toward constructing a portfolio that invests a substantial portion of its assets in real estate. Investing in these types of assets makes it harder for us to get paid, but we believe it is to your economic advantage. Consequently, we created The Wager as a potential Real Advisers revenue stream. As mentioned above, though, there are ways that we can reduce the amount of The Wager, or make it easier to pay over time, or credit all or a portion of it to a trading account for you. The Wager could be invested in an account in your name that Real Advisers will manage for an initial lockup period of three years.

We will explain the necessity for our liquidity restrictions, but it pertains to our projected target returns on your invested funds AND because you, as a client of Real Advisers, will be invested in an illiquid asset class known as "real estate".

I think that we will be incorporating some combination of these options, because in the end, our clients will become our partners and our initial investments in them will be paid back royally.

Chapter 10
The Wager—Part 2

Remember how I mentioned humility? $1,000 per hour is high but it is not the highest rate in the world. There are many people (like Bill Gates) whose hourly rate, the rate of money that they make in an hour, is so high, that I could never afford to pay them for five hours of their time.

Instead, I could make The Offer to Bill Gates and tell him this: "Bill, I am going to donate $5,000 to your foundation, and if you want to know about my thoughts regarding your response to The Task, I'll spend up to five hours discussing it with you. At the end of the discussions, you can pay me whatever amount you want, but no more than five times what I gave your charity, or $25,000. If my ideas give you an idea where you can go and make an immediate $50 million, I won't expect anything more than $25,000 because we want to intentionally set that as a maximum. This is an expression of our humility that we believe is a necessary personality trait for long-term wealth accumulation."

Who may be a better target as a Real Advisers client than Bill Gates is someone in Bill's life, someone he loves who has access to great wealth (maybe even through him), but they remain unhappy and disaffected. They are unfulfilled and are one of those people who may be very rich in financial terms, but they are poor in spirit and isolated. These people may be excellent clients for Real Advisers and may be interested in The Offer.

Chapter 11
Trauma and Psychedelics

The real secret of The Offer, and in fact, the source of your extraordinary value, power, and strength, is that the universe created you just to exist and it delighted in creating you. If the universe enables its intention, your existence is its own justification.

Church of England theologians of the 17th Century wrote about truths of Christianity in the Westminster Confession of Faith, an instructional doctrinal proclamation. Presented in question-and-answer form, the very first question of the Confession is "What is the chief end of man?" The answer is "To glorify God and enjoy him forever". It sounds a little egotistical on God's part doesn't it? Maybe so, but do not forget, God here is defined as the universe. This may be the place where people get too turned off on The Offer, that it is too Christian. I get that. The main point of this paragraph may alleviate your fears: since the "chief end of man" is "to glorify God and enjoy him forever", the purpose of your existence simply is to enjoy life. That is good news for everyone and you do not even have to believe in Jesus for it to be true.

But how do you best enjoy it? Your purpose is to

enjoy life but also to emulate the universe's design. Part of the universe's design is love so part of our enjoyment is related to service. We get additional enjoyment from expressions of our natural inclinations, aptitudes, and curiosities. Having an opportunity to express these things is a wonderful gift.

You may feel, however, like it is impossible for you to ever live in the fullness of the universe's design.

Your expectations are wonderful things and part of your design. God gave you curiosities and inclinations, and we all have a sense that there are high purposes that our lives could fill. Many of us feel discouraged, though, like we will never be satisfied in our careers and that we will always be engaged in a profession or work from which we will never receive fulfillment.

Your expectations and desires should be identified when you are asking the question from The Task about what it is that you want.

Expectations are wonderful because you have the creative potential of the divine inside you. Because of your intrinsic worth that the universe gave you independently of any obligation that you agreed to in exchange, you now have the infinite ability to go out and affect the same divine change on the universe that it exercised by creating you if you follow the maxim: AS ABOVE, SO BELOW.

Where a lot of people get understandably hung up is that they have expectations about their life that do not work out in the way that they think they should. This happens to everybody. I would be surprised if you cannot identify with what I just wrote. If there was somewhere in your life in the past where you wanted something to happen and it did not happen the way that you wanted it to, you probably were disappointed. It may have been an event that was relatively minor, like not being able to go to your first-choice college, or it could have been major where you grew up with a dad who physically abused you.

It could have been severely major if you are a victim of sexual trauma. You had an expectation in your mind that your body and the most intimate part of your being would remain inviolate until such time as you consented to share that with another person. Yet, another person has violated your personal bodily integrity without your permission and has taken what was supposed to be protected. They seized that protected part of your identity from you contrary to your expectations without your consent in a violent or coercive way in total disregard of who you are or what you wanted.

I describe sexual assault in these terms to note that all trauma has to do with a violation of the underlying fundamental expectation of safety that all humans share. It is certainly reasonable to have an expectation of your own personal integrity, safety, bodily security, and privacy. These are fundamental needs and trauma results if these needs are not met.

There is another kind of trauma that creates things like systemic racism. It also creates dysfunctions that we experience in our families. This is intergenerational trauma. Abuse is wrong no matter what, but abusers so frequently were abused themselves by their own parents or others. This is not an excuse for the abuse but a reason for it and an important one to identify.

I may have been so traumatized by something in my upbringing, either from my parents or third parties (pedophiles), that as a result I have PTSD, a disorder that is triggered by ordinary life circumstances. People with PTSD will tell you that it completely debilitates them particularly when they are triggered. A triggering occurs when something in the present that is otherwise innocuous so takes the person back to the place of trauma by association that they relive the trauma in the present. They instantaneously re-experience the deep pain of the injuries to their psyche caused by the trauma. They relive the terror and pain and that triggers a fight or flight response.

A person with PTSD may be confronted with the task of raising their young child. They do their best but they have this severely debilitating condition. A triggering event causes them to act in a way toward their child that has the effect of terrorizing and wounding the child. In the process, the parent creates trauma in the child and PTSD may result. The trauma is passed down through generations.

Because I know about the sexual trauma that my dad experienced as a teenager as the victim of a pedophile athletic coach at his boarding school in the 1950s, I know the hurtful things that he said and did to me resulted from events that triggered his PTSD or out of mental illness that resulted from his PTSD. It makes it easier for me to understand why he acts the way he does sometimes. I have been able to dialogue more with him about these matters over the past few years to our mutual benefit. I love both my parents dearly. In fact, I dedicated this book to my dad and my mom.

One of the things that I would like for Real Advisers to contemplate and take steps to address is intergenerational trauma. As I mentioned, this is expressed directly in dysfunctional families and things like systemic racism, both of which are destabilizing factors for our society.

Unresolved trauma creates mental illness. It creates disruptions in our interpersonal relationships, and it impairs the ability to accumulate wealth on a long-term basis. Everyone has experienced trauma at some point in their lives. Many people can overcome it, but many cannot. We all have heard accounts of people suffering from PTSD who are totally unable to live productive lives as part of a community. Many of the homeless fall into this category.

The good news in all of this is that recently there have been profound and significant advances in the science of using psychedelics to treat mental health disorders, most notably, PTSD.

A long-term vision of Real Advisers is to help create and fund retreats that are specifically targeted at helping people heal trauma. We are doing this in a context of wanting to help people grow and achieve this truly heart-centered wealth that I describe in The Offer. This wealth is based on an infinite personal potential that someone with trauma may be unable to see regarding themselves.

As long as you have unprocessed trauma in your life, you will experience a drag against performance in whatever you are trying to achieve. If you have unprocessed trauma in your life that regularly impairs your ability to earn or save or engage in any of those things that you need to do to trend yourself in the direction of wealth accumulation, your trauma must be dealt with before you can become wealthy.

Our long-term vision at Real Advisers is to help people heal trauma. This chapter is not intended to provide you with all the information necessary for you to evaluate for yourself the relative risks and merits of psychedelics as therapeutic tools. Neither is this medical or legal advice. What I write in The Offer is one man's opinion based on his own personal experience.

In 2012 I was suicidal. I was going through my divorce and I thought that life had lost meaning because my wife no longer wanted to be married to me. I thought that I would be incapable of ever being a blessing to my kids as a divorced dad. I literally thought that the world would be better off without me.

Nevertheless, through Dialectical Behavioral Therapy (after spending about a week in a psychiatric hospital) I found some new hope in a way that I never had before then. Dr. Marsha Linehan developed DBT as a form of cognitive behavior therapy based on Buddhist principles of acceptance and mindfulness. Her story itself is remarkable in how she developed DBT to save herself first, and then employed it to help lots of other people including me (through other therapists)! DBT employs concepts of mindfulness and emotional discipline training. It should be taught in high schools.

The training that I received through this therapy has served me well. I employ DBT's core concepts daily and they are a great help to me (particularly when combined with meditation). In 2012, I was directed on a definite path of recovery and it started with DBT. I emphasize this because some people could read what I write in this book and think that I am saying that psychedelics alone are a quick fix for mental health issues. That is not true.

What psychedelics did for me was to reinforce what I learned in DBT, particularly by allowing me to connect with yoga and meditation in way that I never had.

After I received the DBT therapy, I began to research psychedelics. Prior to that time, I already had experimented with medical cannabis and it had given me great relief from my depressive symptoms, more than anything ever had including numerous prescription psychopharmaceuticals. Some of the most fascinating information I read about psychedelics was research showing that psychedelics (including cannabis) can instigate neurogenesis. Another way of saying this is that ingesting psychedelics can cause you to grow new brain cells.

Of course, in 2012 cannabis and all plant-based psychedelics were illegal to possess in Texas. When you wonder about whether Roland Wiederaenders is a criminal, please remember that by this time, I had spent a week in a psychiatric hospital. In the days before that, I had held a loaded gun to my head, looking in the bathroom mirror where to aim. I was desperate and I was looking for anything that could possibly alleviate my depression and take away my constant suicidal ideations. DBT was helpful but I still struggled.

In late 2012 and into 2013, I had multiple powerful

experiences with psilocybin that were profoundly transformative. My first time consuming four grams of dried psilocybin-containing mushrooms, I experienced an instantaneous shift in my perception. I felt like David writing the Psalms, realizing how God delighted in him and saw him as a beautiful creation independently of anything that David would ever do. Everything was sourced in a creator god that had special awareness of me. I knew what it was like to dance with ecstatic joy before my creator just like David when they brought the ark back to Jerusalem. My experiences with psilocybin (and later Ayahuasca) were among the most immediately transformative ones of my life.

  Despite my disclaimer about psychedelics NOT being a quick fix, research has shown that the positive effects that people experience after having ingested entheogens persist for sometimes months and are observable by their friends and acquaintances. This is significant. It is not just me who has noticed the change. If you know any of my best friends, ask them who Roland was in 2012 and what he was like. They can testify to changes, and I believe that the changes have their source in my experiences with psychedelics. Psychedelics saved my life and I am not the only one who can tell the same story.

Two 2015 Ayahuasca ceremonies were tremendously beneficial to me. In fact, I believe that my T. H. Chalm Bible poetry grew directly out of those two experiences. My poetry is based on books of the Bible, so Ayahuasca drove me artistically to my source, my creator and my God.

The way that this happened was my creation of a backstory for my poetry pseudonym as if "T. H. Chalm" were a real person. In my books, I describe him as an Australian salamander biologist I met at Barton Springs in Austin. In the morning after one of the Ayahuasca ceremonies, I wrote a long poem, "Thucydides Ascending", about Chalm leaving this earthly realm being taken into heaven just like Elijah in a flaming chariot. I describe Chalm as dying in 2015 and leaving behind thousands of unpublished manuscripts to me in trust for publication.

Why is it surprising that a natural psychedelic medicine would lead me back to my source? Ayahuasca is a brew made by boiling leaves and shredded bark of two different species of Amazonian plants. The resulting "tea" contains a natural MAOI inhibitor and DMT in oral form. DMT is dimethyltryptamine, a psychedelic chemical substance naturally occurring in many plants and animals. In fact, we have DMT in our brains, and theories suggest that DMT release in our brains while we sleep is related to dreaming. The natural MAOI inhibitor of Ayahuasca allows the orally ingested DMT to cross the blood-brain barrier, or else it would not otherwise be available to the brain where its therapeutic effects occur.

One of the books of the Bible that my T. H. Chalm poetry re-writes is Ecclesiastes. From that perspective, Ayahuasca led me directly to The Offer.

I can say that the careful, intentional, and responsible use of psychedelics drew me closer to my source. I cannot see how that would not happen through the use of natural medicines fundamentally different from the manufactured prescription psychopharmaceuticals that were my only option for so many years.

When I came back to cannabis in 2008, I found relief in a way that I never had. When I had my experiences with psilocybin in 2012, my depression was altered in a fundamental way for the better. For the first time in my life, I could genuinely identify with the notion of God's love for me. I could FEEL that love. I had the ineffable experience that almost everyone describes when they take psychedelics: the feeling of an unmistakable unifying interconnectedness with the entire universe and a belief that the universe has a benevolence, and that it has a specific awareness of my identity.

Through psychedelics and yoga, I genuinely connected with meditation for the first time in my life. I have only been practicing regular meditation for three and a half years, 15 minutes a day, but even during this short time period, meditation has had a deeply transformative effect on me.

Natural psychedelics have served to reinforce my Christian concept of God, Jesus. I can describe to you in different ways how blessings have flowed from my experiences with psychedelics in 2012 and 2015. My life has grown in abundance in many ways, all culminating in The Offer. The Gospel of Matthew includes a statement from Jesus that even Aleister Crowley agrees with, that "wisdom is proved right by her deeds".

I initially picked MAPS as a charitable organization I wanted to support when in 2012, I read about a study they were conducting using MDMA in connection with marital therapy. A $2,500 donation allowed a married couple to participate in a MDMA-assisted counseling session. When I first read about this therapy, I thought it could have saved my own marriage. This concept inspired me to give and give and continue to give to this great organization. Now in 2020, MAPS funded research that has resulted in the near-FDA approval of MDMA as a therapy for PTSD

    As I mentioned, my intention here is not to present all the scientific information and research that has been done in connection with psychedelics. I am not alone in believing that one of the great crimes against science in the 20th and 21st centuries is that these largely plant-based medicines that are remarkably safe continue to remain among the most highly illegal substances under the U.S. federal Controlled Substances Act, classified as more dangerous than cocaine, heroin, and alcohol. We all know and understand that there has been a major shift in thinking about these substances, yet there are many people in the United States who have no firsthand experience with cannabis and other psychedelics. They believe (many times, with willful ignorance=COGNITIVE BIAS) in the lies of the DARE! and Just Say No! anti-drug programs from the 1980s and 1990s that described cannabis and psychedelics as more dangerous than heroin, meth, or cocaine, and certainly alcohol, which of course is completely legal.

I would challenge anyone to look at Great Britain's leading medical journal, the Lancet, and its 2012 published study classifying the relative risks, harms, and benefits of the most used drugs in the world, including legal drugs like alcohol, caffeine, and nicotine. The study classified the relative harm of illegal "drugs" too, including all of the ones I mentioned above. The Lancet's study concluded that alcohol actually is the most dangerous drug in Britain, more dangerous than heroin or crack cocaine.

Alcohol is a substance that is legal for purchase in some parts of Europe by people as young as 17. Thankfully in the United States you still must be 21 to purchase alcohol. Nevertheless, we all know of the extremely destructive nature of alcohol even when consumed "responsibly". In fact, when you make The Wager and ask me what I think, one of the things I inevitably will discuss with you is your relationship with alcohol. People who abuse alcohol are more likely than not to engage in behavior that will be a drag to their long-term economic performance.

To conclude this chapter, I challenge anybody

who has any doubt about the healing potential of psychedelics to watch the Israeli documentary, Trip of Compassion. This documentary follows the lives of three people who each suffered severe trauma as victims. Nevertheless, they were able to overcome the detrimental effects that the trauma had on their lives because of their PTSD. Through the legal MDMA therapy available in Israel, these individuals conquered their PTSD and went on to lead more fulfilling and impactful lives. The turnarounds their lives experienced from overcoming PTSD demonstrated their renewed ability to cultivate the same characteristics that I describe in The Offer as trending you towards the accumulation of long-term wealth.

 Michael Pollan also has a good book out now that has been getting attention in the popular media called How To Change Your Mind. I highly recommend it.

 Research MAPS, and I strongly encourage you to support MAPS and other organizations like it that are working to demonstrate the clear, scientifically proven, safe, effectiveness of psychedelics as therapeutic tools to overcome mental illness. With further research in the future, other psychedelics will be used in new ways and with similarly remarkable results as MDMA.

Again, this chapter is not intended to be an exhaustive description of the possibilities of psychedelics and does not constitute medical advice. In the Appendix of The Offer you will find references to online bibliographies from several third-party sources (including MAPS) where you can find additional information about psychedelics.

One of the resources listed in the Appendix is the Yale Manual for Psilocybin-Assisted Therapy of Depression. If you are looking for information about how to treat your depression with psilocybin, I believe that this manual could be extremely helpful to you. There are many places on the internet where you can find it but we are making it available through thchalm.com because of how valuable we believe this information is. It is essential information like this that is necessary for desperate people looking to treat depression with an alternative modality that in my experience and in the experience of many others has much higher healing potential than conventional, prescription psychopharmaceuticals.

I believe that a naturally occurring compound like psilocybin will help you reconnect with your identity in a way that is necessary for real healing. I would contrast this with the soul and personality numbing effects of the prescription drugs so frequently prescribed for depression and anxiety that were ineffective for me.

    I want to mention DBT one more time. After the initial intensive, five-week, four night per week, three hours per night intensive session at the Seton Mind Institute in Austin, I followed up with a talk therapist who was trained in DBT counseling methods. He also employed Eye Movement Desensitization and Reprocessing (EMDR), a psychotherapy treatment designed to alleviate the distress associated with traumatic memories. EMDR was beneficial to me as was the talk therapy that reinforced the concepts learned from DBT.

    Both my therapist then (and the psychiatrist I was seeing when I began taking medical cannabis in 2008) were open to my use of cannabis and psilocybin. They of course warned me about the legal issues, but they did not discourage me or tell me that cannabis or psychedelics would be harmful medically or contraindicated by my prescribed medicines. To his credit, my psychiatrist never told me that the psychopharmaceuticals he prescribed were contraindicated by my simultaneous use of cannabis.

This is confirmed in the medical literature. The reason I include this paragraph is to encourage you to discuss psilocybin and other psychedelics with your counselors, therapists, and psychiatrists.

At the same time, I also would strongly encourage you to find another counselor, therapist, or psychiatrist if you believe that resistance to or discouragement of your use of psychedelics is related to antiquated and ignorant notions about the safety of these natural substances.

The same Lancet study that ranked alcohol as the most dangerous drug lists cannabis and psychedelics as about as potentially harmful as caffeine when you take away the potential harm caused simply by the fact that cannabis and psychedelics are frequently illegal to possess.

The pharmaceutical industry is shaking in its boots about psilocybin because they will have a very difficult time making money from a chemical that is so readily available in nature. The same is true with cannabis as medicine. The pharmaceutical industry certainly will do everything they can to discourage mental health workers from taking a favorable stance toward natural psychedelics because that favorable view will hurt the industry's profits.

There are certain instances when psychedelics are not recommended (particularly with people suffering from schizophrenia), but often, you will be discouraged from psychedelics by your mental health professional for the wrong and not the right reasons.

Chapter 12

Your Focus—An Illustration From Freediving

I would recommend that everyone ask themselves where their focus is. Wherever you direct your thoughts, that is the place they will go to, and your reality will arise from that. This is the central tenant of Think And Grow Rich, a book that has blessed me. Think and Grow Rich also demonstrates the Biblical concept that your thoughts create your own reality. I believe this to be true. Think and Grow Rich is so relevant that I devote Chapter 19 of The Offer to a discussion of this classic of self-help literature.

Recently, I spoke with my friend Loïc, a French/Swiss freediving champion and Zen monk, about *presence* in his life, and meditation. We talked specifically about how he uses meditation to compete in freediving, an intense athletic competition that involves underwater breath-hold diving to depths sometimes exceeding 100M for sometimes longer than three minutes. Loïc is supremely conditioned, disciplined, and employs meditation as a tool to help him compete successfully.

Loïc enjoys his life as a freediving instructor on the Red Sea and is a wealthy person. Again, I do not know specifics about his bank account. I have asked him to take his Series 65, join our firm, and become Real Advisers' wealth adviser to freediving tourists in Sharm El-Sheikh. Do you think he is going to be successful? I know he will be because he already is!

Loïc told me about his focus on depth. The freediving competitions are won by people who are able not only to dive the deepest but also return safely to the surface. This is such a critical concept because for self-exploration to be effective, we must go in but then also come back out. We must be relevant to our world to serve our communities.

We must be willing to look deep inside to perform The Task, to be completely honest about all three questions. If you are not honest, you may not uncover a cognitive bias that you have had since an early age that is a direct impediment to your accumulation of wealth. Overcoming that one bias may be the key to you experiencing exponential growth in your life and wealth.

In freediving, even if you achieve your intended depth, you still must safely swim back to the surface holding your breath the entire time. When you are at the surface, you are greeted with a judge who will observe you perform your freediving "task". If you are able to remove your goggles and give the OK sign within a set time (a matter of seconds) after returning to the surface, that is a safe dive and you are given a white card. If you reach the surface and immediately pass out, or because you are gasping for breath, you cannot perform this task, you have not successfully completed the dive. Even though you made it back up to the surface, your dive will be disqualified. (There are safety divers present to bring you up if you pass out before you reach the surface, which happens far too frequently. The sport can be dangerous if performed aggressively.)

Many people might linger at their own depths and maybe are afraid of returning to the surface. This of course is dangerous, and the focus here really is on community. You must go to the depths, but you must not remain there. You must reemerge safely from your depths and re-engage in community.

If you are an introvert like me, this is a challenging notion. One of the blessings to me from meditation, however, has been an expanded empathy. It is much easier for me to be in community now because increased empathy has allowed me to be humbler. I am much more accepting of the people around me and their differences than I ever have been before. I discuss meditation more in Chapters 15 and 16.

My artistic focus (which revolves so much about my identity and wants, and maybe where I can best serve) drove me in a Godward direction and my source (Jesus) places a strong emphasis on the church. Ideally, my community would arise out of my communion with the source. In that way, the community I would be the most intimately engaged with would be a community focused on our source. The message of Christianity is one of forgiveness and redemption. In Christian terms, there is a resurrection here and in the world to come (after death), so the freediving metaphor is directly applicable.

When you explore the depths, you had to confront trauma. Know that when you return from the depths there must be a community of people around you to support you as you continue to process and integrate all of your experiences from your trauma recovery. In the next chapter I describe the force multiplier effect both with draft horses and communities. Because of the force multiplier effect, I encourage you to think about steps you can take to reengage with a community that you already may be a part of, or maybe there is a new community that you could be part of or help create.

Maybe there is an existing faith-based community that would welcome a new member, a new visitor. Even during COVID-19, I have participated in online fellowships, and the love and desire to serve all the wide world was evident even through Zoom. There are many genuinely caring people who have God-given intrinsic desires to bless their world. If you are looking for a community, it is possible to find one. You are looking for a place that can both serve your needs, but you also are looking for a place where you can serve.

You could create your own community. I and two friends created Merciful Gardener Foundation Inc., a Texas tax exempt corporation seeking to provide food and housing to the poor on a sustainable basis. Real Advisers recommends charitable giving to all its clients as a tax management strategy and as a way to shift your focus onto community, to answer how you best can serve. Your life will be blessed, and you will find greater enjoyment from your wealth as you see it being deployed by creating job opportunities for people in your community and funding needs that otherwise would go unmet. Your focus shift will help people, and those people will bless your name for your benevolence. In the words of Russel Brand, "If we don't manifest goodness, who will?"

Community helps give you a focus and helps you determine how you can best serve.

Community is a safe place where you can process trauma. The Ayahuasca ceremony demonstrates both the power of a natural psychedelic and the power of community. After the most powerful mind-altering, medicinal effects of the Ayahuasca begin to subside, you remain together with the same group of people with whom you ingested the medicine, but frequently, you may gather in smaller groups. Everyone was in a very emotionally receptive state and community-focused healing occurred as we talked with each other about life challenges and what the medicine revealed to us about ourselves. True healing occurred for me at the Ayahuasca ceremonies and it was aided not only by the plant medicine but also by the relationships I developed with the other people in attendance. These relationships have continued to be deeply meaningful to me to this day.

Chapter 13

Community and Wants—Horse Force Multiplier Illustration

This chapter illustrates multiple principles of The Offer.

Through Googling, I identified several versions of the following story about draft horses that all express the same fundamental concept. There probably is a scientific study proving the matters I am about to describe, but it also sounds like a common knowledge thing about horses. The claim in these accounts is that, if a single draft horse can pull one unit of weight, then two horses should only be able to pull two units of weight, right?

The narratives love this hook because the surprising answer is "no"! The answer is that the two horses can pull THREE units of weight.

One theory about how the horses can do this is that, because horses are pack animals with an active herd instinct, they are more willing to do certain things together that they would not do alone. When I went swimming in the deep ocean in Hawaii, I was not alone. There were other people with me, so I felt a greater degree of safety than if I were alone even if the actual danger remained the same.

As pack animals, the horses can manifest a different intent in a pair or more of them working together than they can by themselves. They demonstrate a willingness to do things in a group that they are not willing to do alone. They feel safer in their community, and their rest enables their industry. They can rest (somewhat) in their community while working and they intensify their effort over what they could do alone.

Think about how you could employ this force multiplier effect by creating a real estate investment community. If you have a partner, either romantic or otherwise, maybe a friend, you could work together to create functionally your own "multi-family" property by buying a single-family home together. If you view it as an investment going in, have a mechanism to govern disputes and handle liquidity at an agreed-upon valuation (current appraised value), partnerships can work even with joint ownership of something illiquid like a single-family home. With the frequency of divorce, it even may be better for married couples to consider buying their homes together through partnerships. Again, this is not legal advice. I am trying to describe how things *could* be done and how they actually are done by people who are smart enough to educate themselves and work through all of the issues.

Some of these people became clients of mine in my law practice. They grew so effective at forming these partnerships that they banded together to form asset management companies with their closest friends and business partners. Through their asset management companies, they went out to their other wealthy friends who secretly were jealous about the returns in real estate they had been watching my clients achieve over the past few years. My clients eventually ask their wealthy friends, "Would you like to invest?" Then my clients call me for my law firm's services. Their creation of the private securities that their friends invest in necessitates the services of my law practice.

Real Advisers will inform you about different asset classes within commercial real estate. One of the safest to invest in is multi-family, which typically are large apartment complexes. For our purposes, think about properties with more than 100 units. They may be efficiency units, or one- to three-bedroom apartments.

The reason that multi-family is the best asset class on a risk adjusted basis forms the underpinnings of this book. The efficiencies of scale achieved with multi-family properties make it a great investment because of the single fundamental need that all humans share. You will need to lay your head down tonight. It will happen and the only question is, are you going to use that place as an asset or a liability? Remember Robert Kiyosaki? I highly recommend that you read Rich Dad, Poor Dad. It is not a perfect book but this one isn't either. Far from it. We both are trying to make different arguments, though, for why it is such a good idea for people to invest in real estate. The force multiplier effect is at work with multi-family real estate, just like with the horses.

I describe to you in Chapter 15 the 500-person audience that Ryan Gibson of Spartan Investment Group, LLC and I spoke to at the conference in Denver. These people were all attending to learn more about syndicating multi-family investment partnerships. I also describe in this book my client Canis Major Incubator, LLC, a commercial real estate incubator in Austin that is helping people invest in commercial real estate in a similar way as Real Advisers.

By banding together, these clients achieved more together than they could have individually. This was both because of economies of scale and also undoubtedly because they were working together like the horses.

There inevitably is a force multiplier effect of working together with others because of the likelihood that you can manifest an intention to put forth more or better effort than you can or will had you been working on a problem alone.

Chapter 18 is entitled "Diet and Wellness". I discuss in that chapter the importance of yoga, and it's why I invited Aubrey Marcus of Onnit to serve on the Board of Real Advisers. I want people who are focused on health and wellness, because those attributes will trend you in the direction of wealth accumulation.

I mention Onnit because it owns Black Swan Yoga, the yoga studio where I have practice. Like all group fitness and coached exercise, yoga provides a great example of the draft horse, force multiplier effect. Black Swan has multiple locations throughout Austin, and that is a good thing because inconvenience is never an excuse for me not to go. I have been going regularly for the past few years, and the teachers all know me by name.

I love yoga as a moving meditation and an exercise regimen that helps condition my breathing and core for swimming. I am a better swimmer now than ever before because of yoga. One of the reasons that I feel so passionately about yoga (and masters swimming) is the force multiplier effect at work in a group workout setting.

I am willing to do things in class, and expend effort in different ways, that I may not be willing to do alone. I am willing to acknowledge my laziness, but I also assert that I am not strictly like a pack or herd animal like a horse. I have a greater capacity for self-discipline , self-regulation and motivation. I can make myself act as both the horse and jockey. This is a running joke between me and another attorney in Austin with his own practice. When you work for yourself, you have to both be the one who performs the work, and also the one that has to motivate yourself to a higher level of effort. We all have heard the metaphor of "upping your game."

If you want to up your game in any exercise regimen, I highly recommend that you engage that regimen in a group workout context if possible, or with a coach. You will experience gains over what you will if you just work out alone. While a coach or group classes may impose an additional cost or expense that you would rather spend on something else, get in touch with your wants and identity and decide whether that additional cost is worth it to you. It is worth it to me because of the gains. I want to be as fit as my dad at 77 and I joke with him now that I am going to be fitter. I am going to be doing handstands by then. But if this is not important to you, everyone is different. Please just make sure you a trending yourself in the direction of health, however you are doing that. Healthy people are wealthier people and on average, health brings better life enjoyment than money provided that basic needs are met.

Writing The Offer has caused me to "up" my game through a great deal of effort. I expended that effort without the benefit of a herd around me, other than my parents and my artist friends who encouraged me with the poetry. They were my artistic community, and my heart-oriented wealth focuses on art as being a central core of my identity and what I want. I want other knowledgeable people around me to advise me about whether my art is the place where I can best serve.

Chapter 14

Rest—Illustrations From Material Possessions; Titles; Positions

Part of this book talks about why real estate is so important to wealth creation, as it is an investment tool that you can use to meet a fundamental need that you and I and all of humanity share: the need for a safe place to lay our heads at night.

Real estate helps us identify the connection between rest and a material possession. Whatever real estate you have a right to occupy tonight represents an asset (or a potential asset if managed properly) of whoever owns it. This is the case because real estate tends to appreciate in value over time, first. Second, real estate can represent a rental (income) stream for the owner, and the owner can use other real estate to meet their need for a place to stay. These things are obvious, but the importance of these observations is how the notion of rest is related to a physical possession (or at least the right to occupy a physical space) that can be an asset. From Rich Dad, Poor Dad, we know that assets are things that you own that make you money while you sleep.

Everyone knows that they are much more productive the next day after a good night's rest. I guarantee that if you are sleeping under Interstate 35 in downtown Austin tonight, you would sleep far better in the spare bedrooms of my home even if it is a block from the bowling alley. The crashing pins are inaudible from here. The point is that the ability to rest is related to wealth creation.

As wealth advisors, we will give you the basic advice to not spend more than you make, or if you do, make sure you have a good plan. Part of this is the simple advice of creating a budget and our app will include gamifiable budgeting tools that we immediately recommend for ALL our clients, wealthy or struggling. These tools can be used to help our clients determine whether they are spending more than their income, and if so, to show our clients how they frequently can make minor adjustments by focusing specifically on what you want. All things being equal, the more income that you have, you will have greater freedom to enable your desires, and this will allow you to better serve. All of this is all centered around the notion of rest and connecting rest to a physical asset.

Real Advisers will advise you to use real estate as

an investment tool while creating a genuine place of rest for yourself. I want to share a little about how I designed a place of rest for myself over the past few years in the home where I live. This story explains how I rationalized a luxury purchase and describes how you can make this decision for yourself with respect to your own wants.

The house where I live was listed on the Multiple Listing Services, or "MLS", the closest thing to a public marketplace that exists for retail sales of single-family homes. I found it and recommended to my mom that she purchase it so that I could lease it from her as her captive and interested tenant. I thought that this house represented a great buy. My friend James Hill, the real estate agent and professional writer who helped me formulate some of the concepts of this book, was the real estate agent who represented my mom in her purchase.

One of the reasons that I was convinced that this house had such great value potential was the horrible green carpet in the front living room. When the house was on the market, the carpet was the first thing anyone noticed when walking through the front door. Though the owners tried to clean it, it was worn and stained in places. For anyone buying the home, the carpet would be the first thing to go.

I had a vision. My ideal floors were stained concrete. As soon as we bought the house, I was going to tear out any flooring and polish and stain the concrete slab. I never had lived in a home with concrete floors, but I had seen them many places since they had become an imminently practical and fashionable design element in modern residential housing. I really liked their clean and industrial aesthetic. My vision was to have stained concrete floors, and I wanted to buy Persian hand knotted rugs to lay on top of them as a perfect offset.

With the Tax Code's accelerated capital asset depreciation rules, I decided to retrofit the entirety of my home office with rugs in every room. I identified a warehouse business in Austin where a man was selling vintage (and new) hand knotted rugs to clients like Google. I bought five rugs from Kevin, and every time I look at them on my floors, with their intricate floral patterns I am convinced were inspired by psychedelics, I smile. These are physical objects that genuinely give me a sense of peace, rest, and joy.

This is exactly the sense that my dad describes having with his truck. He told me he feels wealthy when he drives his truck. It represents a means to get him to the place (the baseball diamond) where he experiences the greatest agency (and possibly highest current economic potential) as an umpire. This notion of connecting rest and agency to a physical object applies similarly to him.

This is even further illustrated by my friend Sarah "Agent Red" Johnston who is setting out on an adventure with van life. She is becoming super economical as she will both have a means of transportation and a place to sleep. I envy Red and while I think that an apartment is ideal for me, a tricked-out Sprinter van may be preferred. Think of the great variety of beaches I could access!

The principle is the same, in that in this chapter, I am pointing out the connection between rest and physical possessions.

I want to encourage myself, so I go to the mall and buy myself a new necktie. A woman goes to the store to buy new perfume. The couple purchase the painting that they have been admiring in the gallery. They hang it on their wall and every time they look at it, it gives them pleasure. We find pleasure in beautiful things, right? And there is absolutely nothing wrong with that. Our desire for beauty is an inherent human characteristic, right? The idea here is that rest is connected to physical objects that you may buy (or you may not). Get in touch with your wants and what really makes you happy. What do you want? is the central question of The Task.

Answering this question is very helpful for budgeting, so release those subscriptions or unnecessary men's neckwear purchases that direct income away from wealth generating assets. New rugs like the ones I bought can sell for up to $10,000 or more. One of the rugs I bought cost $1,000. It is a vintage (used) rug and is probably older than me. The amount I spent on the rug is more than the $300 that I might have spent at Home Depot for the machine-tufted rug that strictly would have met my needs.

After researching and thinking about it for a long time, I really loved that each of the rugs I bought would be hand-made, and in my mind would possess superior beauty and durability over the rugs at Home Depot. I determined that it was worth it to spend the extra $700 on something that people may see as extravagant but note the following. Remember I'm happy living in an apartment (even though I now happen to live in a house) but my dad wants the "extravagant" luxury of a garden around his home. That extra land around his home (if it were in Austin at least) might cost a lot and to me would not be worth it. But to my dad, it provides him rest and should be budgeted for in his personal heart-centered wealth creation plan. Everyone is different and their answers to The Task will reveal information about how they should use their real estate to create rest for themselves as well as making it an investment tool.

Your appreciation of beautiful things does not have to be an obsession, and you can acquire luxury items and be consistent with the ideas of The Offer. Remember, though, that owning beautiful things comes with a price and an attachment. Many people do not think that as soon as they buy the valuable painting, they should probably add a rider on their homeowners' insurance to cover theft of that painting specifically. That additional monthly expense associated with your ownership of a luxury good is recurring if you own the painting (or at least display it in a location from where it can be stolen). Make sure you keep those nice things you have safe. Real Advisers can help you with your insurance needs.

There is another related matter to the connection between rest and possessions. There is an idea that having a title is a kind of backstop. I can tell you that I earned a JD (a Juris Doctorate), and that says that I went to law school.

Everyone is always so impressed by lawyers for some reason. Attorneys generally are intelligent and articulate, but they also can be some of the most reprehensible people on the planet. This is the case because they literally can interfere with the proper administration of justice and work against the best interests of their clients and others (including minor children who may be subject to a family law matter), all to their profit. The Bible includes numerous condemnations about exploiting the courts, abusing power, and abusing the poor. Also see Jesus' Seven Woes To The Pharisees and Sadducees from the Gospel of Matthew.

Whenever I use "JD" or "Attorney at Law", I derive instantaneous credibility (or maybe scorn) based solely on a title that society recognizes as somewhat impressive or prestigious (or infamous). If I am honest, I must admit the artificial nature of the rest provided by my title because of how little my title has to do with what kind of a human being I really am. Do I know who I am? Have I asked what I want? Do I know how I can serve?

If you are an MD, you are a doctor, and that is impressive to me. I know the difficulty of the science and math that doctors must learn. These were subjects with which I always struggled. If you are Assistant to the Regional Manager, that is a title that has *some* significance and carries with it a minimal amount of authority and gravamen (even though it is also a little joke). Nevertheless, my point is that even something as minor as a title can provide rest.

Have I ever enjoyed that people were impressed with my title? For sure. Have I ever enjoyed the instantaneous credibility that results when people introduce you as a lawyer or even better, "my lawyer". My brilliant economist, photographer, and art dealer friend, Jon Garza of Austin Real Estate Photography, tells his friends that he beats his lawyer at chess regularly (which is only true about three out of every 10 games).

Notice I used "Esq." after my name on the cover. Do you think I did not do that intentionally? It looks a little pretentious normally, but on a book cover it could be deemed somewhat mysterious or prestigious, and it certainly denotes that the person is an attorney if you read it literally. Some people use it after their names to sound sophisticated even if they are not attorneys, but I really am. My Texas State Bar card number is 24008276. Nothing in this book should be construed as legal advice.

Understand that we all have little attachments to the titles, recognize how artificial and silly those attachments are (Asst. to the Regional Manager vs. Asst. Regional Manager), but also understand that titles can be used as temporary tools to create rest, even if the rest is artificial and fleeting.

Remember my want about getting an MFA. I want all those smart professors out there to start reading my poetry with the knowledge that I subjected myself to a specific and recognizable educational program to obtain that degree. That gives my poetry credibility to the professors, but it does not make my poetry intrinsically better.

Sometimes, you need whatever tool will work or be most effective for you. Being an attorney has opened lots of doors to me that otherwise would have been shut. Those open doors have trended me in the direction of long-term wealth creation. Take every opportunity you have to advance your interests, what you want, in a way that advances the creation of true heart-centered wealth in a community-oriented way, and you will be a blessed person. You will both possess wealth and enjoy it too.

My dad illustrates the point about title and position well. He has the title and position of umpire so that gives him instantaneous authority (agency) in the baseball game. He enjoys the immediate credibility when he walks onto the field literally as armored as the catcher. His protective gear is necessary. With every pitch of the game, he must take up a post right behind the catcher, positioning his head as closely behind the catcher's mitt as possible to call balls and strikes accurately. His face is guarded by the metal frame of his mask, and he wears a chest protector, shin guards, and cup. Nevertheless, he has shown me many bruises that he received from errant fastballs, foul balls, and other deflections of pitches uninterrupted by the catcher's mitt that hit unprotected parts of his body.

My dad enjoys being a baseball umpire. Because of how stressful I know it can be, working as an umpire would literally be one the last things on my list of enjoyable things to do. Being an umpire, and exercising the agency that comes with that, and participating in a singular way in an activity that a lot of other people are participating in, enjoying and watching, are perfect examples of my dad's rest. He loves umpiring. I know he is physically exhausted and sometimes severely bruised after umpiring, but I know too that his spirit is soaring because he was engaged in something that he loves. He knows how to create rest through industry, and that his umpiring is rest for him enables him to work hard and enjoy his toil. When you combine rest with industry, you are working on a passion, something that you love, and the work seems effortless. My dad knows how to work hard, and he works hardest at the things he loves the most, umpiring, woodworking, and gardening. My dad is a wealthy man.

Do you have an association with wealth through your car like my dad? He associates wealth with his truck. He even told me he loves the smell of it when he gets in. It is a simple pleasure and partly arises from another source of the great wealth he has. He drives hundreds of miles to baseball fields throughout north Texas from his home near Waco to work as a baseball umpire. He said specifically that his truck and driving it made him feel wealthy. This is the area in his life where he has authority and agency. The umpire, along with the coaches and the players, is one of the participants in the game! Agency is our ability to exercise our divinely-inspired creative drives.

My dad told me his hourly rate was $10 per hour. With his Master of Divinity degree, his rate should be $250 per hour on a part time basis because he could make The Offer to pastors and talk to them in a way that I could not. He can identify with their struggles in a way that I could not. He could be a financial advisor to them in a way that I could not. I just realized that he could be a financial advisor to umpires. Many of his friends are Christians as well, and he could proudly give a copy of The Offer to his friends, or encourage them to download the app so they can participate in a Bible study based on Ecclesiastes that can help them grow rich. This is my hope for The Offer.

Chapter 15
Meditation—Part 1

I must relate to you the following unflattering story of how I came to be such a strong believer in meditation as a wealth creation tool. This demonstrates how in my professional career, I was exercising great agency in an area where I had terrific potential, but I was still cobbled by unresolved trauma from my divorce. This chapter ends on a happy note because I reveal how meditation helped me become a better public speaker. I also describe in this chapter and the next about how meditation has put me on a path of healing the damaged relationship I have with my ex-wife.

In 2017, I was experiencing some great success in my solo law practice. I was gaining clients solely through word-of-mouth, and many clients encouraged me by telling me what great value my services were. I was billing at $350 an hour, and I realized that I could achieve a comfortable income for myself by billing far less than 40 hours per week. As an attorney, you never bill for every hour you work, so billing for me at 40 hours per week probably would require me to work 80+ hours. This is not unusual. Attorneys, whether they are solo practitioners or working at big firms, can work a lot.

This is true of most professionals.

In 2017, a friend and client extended an invitation to me to join as a partner in a company that was going to serve as the asset manager to one or more real estate investment funds. Does that sound familiar? Adventum Funds was a direct conceptual precursor to Real Advisers for me.

Adventum comprised a team of several people filling different roles. Marc was a commercial real estate broker and developer; Lorie (the only woman on the initial team) was an accounting professional; and Eddie was a member of the Texas House of Representatives who had strong ties in the commercial real estate community through his full-time employment at a title company. A fourth member of the team was a gentleman named Saurabh who had grown up in Tanzania but attended college in Wisconsin on a math scholarship. He had several successful software and technology related companies and now was engaged in investing in Austin commercial real estate. I served as their in-house attorney as general counsel, a role that I loved. This team had great potential for me, and I was optimistic as I believed this was finally how God was going to allow me to become a wealth manager on a full time basis and quit my law practice.

This team had great potential for me and even an express "no assholes" policy. I loved it.

The problem for me was that I faced a true impediment to my success. My divorce (commenced in 2011 but finalized in 2013) left me with some major anger issues toward my ex-wife and a skewed view toward women. I resented that Aricka initiated the divorce, and refused counseling, and refused attempts to reconcile, after she realized that our sixteen-year marriage was done. Her desire to end our marriage was justified.

While I never "cheated" on Aricka, I was never present emotionally with her during our marriage. My anxiety and depression interfered with my ability to engage with her emotionally and create intimacy. My sexual relationship with Aricka was negatively impacted by my mental health issues because we never achieved true, consistent, emotional intimacy. While I never had an extra-marital affair, I turned to pornography and masturbation as sexual outlets, and Aricka understandably perceived this as cheating on my part.

In 2011, after my best friend, Mike, committed suicide in January and a major verbal altercation with Aricka before I left work on March 1st, I decided that I was going to leave her and the kids and stay at Mike's house (that I inherited from him) for a while. I slept in my dead friend's bed that night and never felt so alone. Aricka and our four children continued to live in our home over the next year. I would return there in the evenings after my work as in-house counsel at a public pension fund in Austin to help her with our kids with dinner, homework, bathing, and bed. After we put our kids to bed, I drove back across town to stay at Mike's. Aricka and I interacted as childcare workers for our kids, not as husband and wife, and she refused any dialogue with me about how to repair our marriage, understandably so.

Aricka eventually filed for divorce and moved out of our house with the kids into a nearby three-bedroom apartment. When they moved there, I was no longer welcome to visit the place where my children lived with their mom, and it was then when our separation really was complete. Our divorce was finalized about a year later in 2013.

As I mentioned elsewhere in the chapter about trauma, it was at this time in my life when I was at my lowest. Some truly positive things began happening in my life in 2012 and I describe those occurrences elsewhere, but one thing that I never specifically sought to overcome was my anger toward Aricka. While I had been able to identify and acknowledge so much about specifically how I contributed to our divorce, I remained angry at Aricka for what I perceived was her unreasonable unwillingness to attempt reconciliation. The attempt would have been at least our fourth or fifth during our marriage (as we had attended counseling before). Aricka was traumatized, exhausted, and convinced that I would never change. I was convinced of that too and that was why I was suicidal in 2012.

2012 was my bottom, but it also was one of my best years ever in the sense that it was in October 2012 when I had my first powerful experience with psilocybin. Yet, despite all the positive things that took place in my life between 2012 and 2017, in 2017, I still suffered from residual anger toward Aricka.

I was otherwise "successful", but I was continuing to let some of my unprocessed trauma hold me back from developing my true potential.

While we were forming the Adventum team, I initially was optimistic about our chances for success. The team was focused, the investment thesis was sound, and we had genuine ideas for creating significant value.

I really liked the "no assholes" rule until I discovered that I was the asshole. My discovery happened like this.

We selected a two-person board made up of one woman and one man, Marc and Lorie. I knew Marc well and met Lorie through Marc. Lorie was an accountant and had years of experience serving as comptroller and CFO of a real estate fund asset management company in Dallas. Lorie was very competent and because reporting is so important in investor relations, she was one of the most crucial members of our team.

The problem for me was that she really reminded me of Aricka. Innocent things that Lorie would say in meetings or in emails would grind and grate on my nerves. I was convinced that she was intentionally pushing buttons to manipulate my responses. I had a truly skewed view of Lorie in all my interactions with her and it was all completely fueled by my unacknowledged residual anger toward Aricka. I am writing this as an apology to Lorie even though I apologized to her at the time for the one event that revealed to me the depth of my anger, and my need for some tool to help me remedy my continuing struggle with emotional dysregulation.

The event was simply Lorie sending out an email

request for me to perform some work as the firm's attorney. For whatever reason, I interpreted her email as a slight, that she was being "bossy", and I replied by email in an unkind and unprofessional way. Later the same day, I realized that I had responded as an asshole would, violating the team's central rule, and apologized to Lorie for my unkind response. I was so ashamed by my behavior (which in one respect could be characterized as minor) that I felt like I could not continue on the team. I resigned from my position as general counsel to a cool Austin-based real estate investment fund. I had lost an opportunity to become successful because the trauma from my unresolved anger at Aricka had been (mildly) triggered.

After this happened, the other team members expressed understanding as I at least was able to describe my emotions well enough to inform them that the issue was with me, not Lorie. At the time, I told them that I simply could not continue on because of my personal issues.

Saurabh and I spoke after this happened and he was sympathetic. When Saurabh and I spoke, he asked me a question that no one ever had asked me before: "Do you meditate?" I had taken up a yoga practice, attending the Black Swan studio near my house with great regularity, and I had the DBT mindfulness training, so I said this to him in reply: "I consider myself a pretty mindful person and regularly practice yoga." Saurabh persisted though and said: "No, do you meditate?" and I was forced to say no. My curiosity was piqued. My real response was "no, do you?" and he proceeded to tell me about his practice. He said that he had learned Transcendental Meditation and it had been a great tool for him to cope with grief after his mother's death. As I got to know Saurabh better, he told me the remarkable story of his mother's life and her courage and persistence as a schoolteacher who undertook extraordinary measures to obtain a first-rate education for him in Tanzania. I told Saurabh that to redeem my recent embarrassment with Lorie, I needed to make some real change. I committed to him to begin a meditation practice and that I would specifically seek out Transcendental Meditation (TM).

After learning that it cost $1,000 to learn TM, I found Professor Michael Olpin's free video on YouTube entitled "Wellness – How to Meditate". Professor Olpin teaches at Weber State University in Utah and this video was taken of his lecture on wellness to incoming freshman. He says in the video that among the healthiest things that you can do for yourself are to meditate and practice yoga. I could not agree more.

If you want a simple instructional video for a mantra meditation practice, I could not recommend this video more highly. In my practice, I too have adopted Professor Olpin's mantra, the word "still". While this is the mantra that Professor Olpin describes in his video, he says you can use any powerful, significant, or meaningful word. My mantra is a one-word prayer: "Be <u>still</u> and know that I am God", which from my source text is a message of the divine communicating to his creation that we should recognize his providence and get more in tune with his design. In doing so we align ourselves with the universe's intent and its power begins to flow through you. AS ABOVE, SO BELOW.

With meditation, I sit silently with my thoughts for fifteen minutes every day, almost always in the morning. I have established regularity in my morning routine. I get up, begin making coffee and during that time, hydrate with water and ascorbic acid (Vitamin C) sweetened with Stevia. I take my Magnesium Taurate supplement, sit down, enjoy my coffee and water, and scroll headlines on Reddit. After a while, my bowels will begin to feel the effects of the coffee and re-hydration. I meditate immediately after going to the bathroom.

For fifteen minutes I sit on the floor in my bedroom with my eyes closed and focus on the word "still" as my mantra. As Professor Olpin describes, your thoughts will wander. My thoughts always go to my work, my kids, things I am concerned about, things I'm looking forward to, but all of these thoughts are re-directed back to the word "still" as the singular focus of the practice for those fifteen minutes. Whenever I realize that my attention and thoughts have wandered, I immediately bring them back to the mantra. There is no real purpose to this exercise other than to focus and direct your mind on the mantra for an extended period. The regular, daily aspect of the practice is extremely important. TM recommends twice daily, morning and afternoon, twenty minutes per session.

During my times of meditation, sometimes strong emotions come up, but I must sit in silence and experience them. I cling to my mantra at those times as these emotions can be attached to powerful regrets associated with failures in my life. I have experienced some great failures, and my divorce was my greatest. Aricka and I, like almost all people when they get married, said the words "'till death do us part." What parted Aricka and I was divorce, and at the time, I rather would have been dead than experience the pain that our separation caused. I have spent time in meditation weeping at the emotional pain but clinging to my one-word prayer as a life raft. It genuinely helps.

After practicing meditation for a time, I realized some positive effects. First, I felt my empathy expanding in a way that I never had before, and simultaneously I began identifying the anger that I was continuing to carry toward Aricka. Just being able to say in a mindful way that you are cobbled by anger is the first step in overcoming it.

I had denied my anger to myself, another lie. Remember what I said to Saurabh: "I consider myself a pretty mindful person and I practice yoga." The implication was that meditation was not necessary for me, a lie that I was telling myself because I had always been challenged by the thought of meditation and had never really understood or been able to connect with it. To prove myself worthy to Saurabh, though, I committed to him to make a renewed effort. I am so thankful that I did, and I have told Saurabh that he is a *bodhisattva* to me. He laughed.

After practicing regularly for at least six months, I realized how to use my mantra word, "still", during the day to manage anxiety even when I was not actively meditating. What I noticed was that I could be going about my business throughout the day and simultaneously think of the word "still" in my mind. This could happen while swimming, while eating, while meeting with a friend, while reading an email, while drafting a contract, or while driving. Whenever I think of the word specifically, speaking it in my mind, I experience what is now a predictable physiological response. Whenever I focus on the word "still" even momentarily, a wave of calm washes over me. I feel it physically descend from the top of my head down to my gut.

This has never been so perfectly illustrated to me than when I employed this technique to manage anxiety in a situation that would cause GREAT stress for anyone.

If you ask most people to list their greatest fears, public speaking inevitably will appear close to the top. In 2016, I had my first opportunity for a public speaking engagement where I was invited to present a basic overview of corporate and securities law to a group of real estate entrepreneurs at Phill and Shenoah Grove's Real Estate Networking Club. Since that first engagement, I continued to take advantage of other public speaking opportunities until in 2018 I had the chance to speak before a national audience in Denver. The event was a conference sponsored by Joe Fairless, "The Best Ever Conference", where 500 ambitious men and women came together to learn more about syndicating, as issuers, sponsors and promoters of private securities, multi-family real estate investment opportunities. All of these people are perfect potential Real Advisers clients and were and are also perfect potential clients for my law practice.

  The structure of the talk in Denver was a "fireside chat" between an investment manager, Ryan Gibson, CIO of Spartan Investment Group, LLC in Seattle, and me. We discussed "The Unknown Unknowns of US Securities Law." Ryan is the type of manager and Spartan is the type of fund where Real Advisers will direct our clients' investments.

  This speaking engagement was an experience just like you may imagine. When it came time for our talk, we approached the stage from behind a curtain. Friendly applause greeted us as we walked across the stage to take our designated places. There was a couch and a chair where we sat, and everything went completely according to plan. Ryan and I had rehearsed a little beforehand, but we were so well-versed in our respective subject matters that we were able to pull off a naturalistic and informative talk. I even shared something spontaneously about a passion for creating affordable housing for my artist friends.

While we had great success, do you think that I was nervous beforehand? YES! Immediately before we walked out on the stage, I experienced some massive stage fright and anxiety. This was maybe less than a year after I had started meditating and this was one of the first instances of having this experience that I described above about using my mantra as a "waking"-moment method to calm my nerves. Immediately before the curtains were drawn back for us to go out on the stage, at the moment of my highest anxiety, I said the word "still" in my mind with intention, and the same powerful calming wash that I just felt now when I wrote the word on this page came over me then. My anxiety, stage fright, and nervousness mostly disappeared.

When Ryan and I reached our respective places and sat down, I noticed something remarkable. What I observed in Ryan was something that surprised me but that was entirely understandable under the circumstances.

What I noticed was that Ryan was nervous too. It was only noticeable to me, though, because I was able to quell my own nervousness sufficiently to maintain a degree of circumspection. I was able to enter the mindset of an observer. This was so noteworthy to me because it was an unusual experience for me personally.

In reality, I suffer from deep-seated insecurities. Growing up and earlier in my professional career, I frequently assumed that EVERYONE around me was more competent, more intelligent, somehow more worthy. I frequently still suffer from the impostor syndrome, a "psychological pattern in which an individual doubts their skills, talents or accomplishments and has a persistent internalized fear of being exposed as a 'fraud'" (from Wikipedia). When I saw Ryan was nervous, it was only remarkable for me because I remembered specific instances in the past where I simply could not have observed that fact. The emotional stress of the situation would have blinded me from having any objectivity. Noticing another person's nervousness might have caused me to panic.

At that moment, however, I was not so bound to the self-limiting mindset I inhabited in the past. The mindset of the observer moved me forward in the task at hand. I was demonstrating the trait of perspicacity. It was not that I was taking pleasure in seeing that Ryan was nervous. What was significant is that instead of responding with panic, I was reassured that there was another credible person with me in this endeavor who was having the same normal, psychological response as me. This experience would have been stressful for anyone. Nevertheless, my objectivity, and the presence and perspicacity that Ryan also possessed helped us perform in spite of our understandable but momentary fears.

The most important message from this story is not our fear of public speaking, but how Ryan and I moved forward together to accomplish something that 99% of humanity would have a degree of apprehension to even attempt. I acknowledged his nervousness, managed my own, but we moved forward together. Maybe we were like the draft horses? As we proceeded in our talk, I do not think it could have gone any better. Other people told me it was great. A video of our chat is available on YouTube and at QuetzalHiloco's website (thchalm.com). My experience with using my mantra to quiet my nerves at a time when I noticed that someone as highly credible as Ryan was nervous was significant.

I knew that I had discovered a tool that had deep relevance for me. I knew that if I wanted to continue to get in front of audiences and use public speaking to promote myself and my business interests, I would always have my mantra as a place that I could go to whenever those inevitable feelings of anxiety arose. This tool would be available to me at any time in the future when I might speak in front of an audience. (In addition to meditation, I have other specific ideas about training you for public speaking.)

If you begin to implement what we are talking about in this book, you will begin to find yourself in a leadership position in your community, and people will want to know what you think. Begin preparing yourself now to overcome this understandable fear of public speaking that almost all of humanity shares.

As I continued with my regular practice of meditation, one day I remembered a pithy saying that allowed me to get to a place of beginning to release anger toward Aricka. I referenced this saying before, and you probably have heard it: "Anger is the poison that you drink but you expect the person at whom you are angry to die". In meditation, I identified that I would allow my thoughts to run wild in an undisciplined way whenever I would think about Aricka. I realized that when I was undisciplined in that way, I would allow my angry thoughts to feed on themselves, only increasing the sickness that I had inside myself that I thought I was creating for Aricka. The true blessing though was realizing that it was entirely optional for me to drink the poison. I could decide whether to drink it or not.

    What I began doing is confronting the angry thoughts with the reality and truths that I knew were factual. I started an inner dialogue about how Aricka was an excellent and caring mom to our kids (she is), and how she possessed so many admirable qualities. I would direct my thoughts to how she was such a blessing to our kids whom we both love so much and want nothing else than to be a blessing to their lives. I wanted to begin to train myself to think of Aricka in a different way. Meditation has helped me do this and while I still suffer from angry intrusive thoughts, I confront these thoughts with the truth that I do not have to engage them. The counter thoughts are the reminders I can give myself about Aricka's excellence, and how she blesses our kids, the same people that both Aricka and I love the most out of anyone in the world. In the next chapter, I describe a specific new loving-kindness mantra I have adopted to counter my intrusive angry thoughts more specifically.

What this chapter illustrates is that I had a perfect opportunity in 2017 to work with what seemed to be the perfect team to advance a goal of mine that had existed since 2004. My continuing anger toward Aricka was an impediment to me capitalizing on that opportunity, but from my failure and interaction with Saurabh, I gained meditation, and that led me to The Offer.

Chapter 16
Meditation—Part 2

Meditation is so essential that I decided to include a second chapter about it in The Offer! This chapter discusses my use of meditation to further overcome the anger at my ex-wife, Aricka, that I described in the last chapter.

Writing The Offer has been a cathartic experience for me. To describe my past accurately, I have had to admit some uncomfortable truths about myself. I confess that I do not have perfect understanding of all my personal dysfunctions, neuroses, and cognitive biases. Nevertheless, the process of writing accurately about my life experiences forces me to examine my shortcomings more closely. That is frequently an emotionally difficult task.

While the truths about myself that I write about in The Offer are sometimes personally embarrassing, I have described them here with the goal of wanting to help people become wealthy. The reason why I think The Offer is so worthwhile, and why I have shared so much about my personal experience is because I know my experiences are not unusual. While my details are specific to me, things that happened to me in my marriage and divorce are things that happen to everyone. Everyone grows up with unrealistic views of romantic relationships, and everyone at some level can understand the incredible pain of separation from someone that you love (or once loved in a different way). Everyone will experience trauma at some point in their life.

Toward the end of the last chapter, it sounded like I completely overcame those angry intrusive thoughts toward Aricka, right? Do you think that is true? Sadly, it is not.

While I wrote The Offer, I adopted a second meditation practice to combat my continuing angry thoughts toward Aricka. In addition to the fifteen minutes I spend with my meditation practice in the morning (employing my mantra word, "still"), I have adopted a separate fifteen-minute loving-kindness meditation practice for my afternoons. I try to establish regularity in this practice by starting as close to noon or after lunch as possible every day.

I direct my practice toward myself first, and then toward Aricka and her second husband of nearly two years, Charles, simultaneously. I direct the practice at myself first because I must have loving-kindness for myself. Without loving myself, I will be cobbled in how

I can love others. If I cannot perceive myself as the universe perceives me, then I am perceiving myself and my abilities inaccurately. I want to live in reality. I do not want to be bound by my cognitive biases and self-limiting beliefs. I want to live in the fullness of love that I know the universe has for me. I want to live in the fullness of love that I know the universe has for everyone, including Aricka.

I want to love others like Jesus loved me. Love is incredibly hard sometimes, and in fact when Jesus tried it, the religious authorities and government officials crucified him because he represented such an existential threat to their power structures. I believe that love can be a tremendously destabilizing force for the self-limiting power structures created when we engage in anger.

The loving-kindness that I direct toward myself in this meditation is articulated by these traditional prayers and mantras:

May I be filled with loving-kindness.
May I be safe from inner and outer harm.
May I be well in my body and in my mind.
May I be at peace and be happy.

These are not magic words, and they could change over time. Essentially, I am asking for blessings for myself that everyone wants from the universe. Love, health, well-being, safety from harm, and peace are the essential components of these blessings.

The next step is directing these thoughts toward the world:

May all people be filled with loving-kindness.
May all people be safe from inner and outer harm.
May all people be well in their body and in their mind.
May all people be at peace and be happy.

Finally, in my meditation, I narrow the scope to those people toward whom I experience the most anger, Charles and Aricka:

May Charles and Aricka be filled with loving-kindness.
May Charles and Aricka be safe from inner and outer harm.
May Charles and Aricka be well in their body and in their mind.
May Charles and Aricka be at peace and be happy.

During the short time I have engaged in this practice, I nearly always take the next step and direct these messages toward our children. This is the case because I love our children, of course. This has relevance for Charles and Aricka, though, because they are both loving parents. (Charles is a widower and has children from his prior marriage.) I know that Aricka delights in her children like most mothers. She derives deep joy and life satisfaction from her relationship with them. For her to be at peace and to be happy is to have peaceful and happy children who have peaceful and happy relationships with her. I know that Charles feels the same way about his children.

When I recite these mantras, sometimes I visualize how Charles and Aricka are spending time together with our children, laughing, enjoying a shared experience, or simply sitting together reading books or watching a movie. I see images in my mind of them at peace and at ease and completely content. That is what I want.

Through this process I have understood much more what Jesus meant when he told us to love our enemies. This is such a radical concept. Charles and Aricka certainly are not my enemies but sometimes because emotions run so high and because my anger is so intense it feels like they are. Jesus' command to love our enemies is easy to obey with respect to Charles and

Aricka because we have so many common interests (our children) and because we once actually were friends at church (even though conflicts have taken a severe toll on our relationships). Despite the conflicts and anger that I feel toward them, I could never say that Charles and Aricka are my enemies. I genuinely want them to be friends again, and that is why I adopted this second meditation practice. I want to completely rid myself of all anger that I continue to carry toward them, and I want to engage in a regular focused practice that is intended to bless myself and them. Do you carry irrational anger toward anyone? Do you carry rational anger toward anyone?

Whenever I have an angry intrusive thought during the day, I speak my loving-kindness mantra.

I include this second chapter on meditation in The Offer first, because meditation is so important, but second, because I wanted to describe to you how I was seeking to release anger toward the person in my life with whom I have had the greatest conflict, my ex-wife. Can you relate?

It is unsurprising that we have conflict. We once were in love, committed our entire lives and futures to each other, but then later rejected those earlier commitments in exchange for a divorce. The road from marriage to divorce frequently is paved with conflict. This is not unusual or surprising.

What I want to be surprised about in my experience with divorce are the results of the meditation practice I describe in this chapter. In some ways, I do not know how I can ever be friends with Aricka and Charles again. We have some radically different beliefs, particularly about the advisability and safety of the use of cannabis and psychedelics. It may surprise you that in 2020 this is a point of conflict between us because of how society's views toward cannabis and psychedelics have shifted so dramatically.

Nevertheless, many people continue to be concerned about legal issues surrounding cannabis and psychedelics. They remain illegal to possess in many jurisdictions, but in the United States we truly are witnessing the dying throes of the War on Drugs. Independent of the legal issues, very conservative Christians believe that ingesting cannabis and psychedelics are the same thing as sorcery and in one specific sense they are correct. If I am attempting to commune with demons or spirits, that is the definition of sorcery, a practice condemned by Christians. I would like to write another book about the relationship between Christianity and psychedelics. I highly recommend a book on this topic that already has been written, The Immortality Key by Brian C. Muraresku (who also happens to be an attorney). Brian describes the "continuity hypothesis" that links the ancient Greek Dionysian Mystery rights from the Temple of Eleusis (which certainly involved the ritual use of natural psychedelics) to the early adoption and practice of Christianity immediately after the time of Jesus.

Conflicts over beliefs about anything, including cannabis and psychedelics, never become so evident or seem more important when they relate to our religion or politics. Conflict also arises strongly when we disagree about how to communicate our beliefs to our kids and how we train them in right behavior and morals. This is the case because caring parents usually have strongly held beliefs about what is best for their children. All parents have responsibilities for communicating morals and training behavior in their children. Communicating beliefs and training our kids about "drugs" has been a major point of contention between Aricka and me.

Nevertheless, I believe that I can train my heart to expand in the direction of Charles and Aricka. Why am I doing this? Remember how my meditation starts. I must love myself before anyone else. I am taking this focused action to release my anger because every ounce of my energy spent toward feeding anger is wasted. There exists the concept of effectiveness, which is simply the most efficient direction of energy toward a goal. If you continue to carry anger in your heart, if you continue to direct energy toward feeding anger like I do too frequently, that anger is going to be a detractor from your ability to accumulate wealth. You will be devoting time to an unproductive activity. You will be ineffective. Please join me in giving up the hobby of anger. I am taking specific steps to release mine and I would strongly encourage you to do the same. In fact, if you accept The Offer and you hear what I think about your answers to the questions of The Task, I will direct you to this chapter if you tell me about continuing anger in your life. Know that you are not a victim to anger, and you can take specific steps to overcome it. You also are not alone. Everyone experiences anger.

  To conclude this second chapter on meditation, I would emphasize that there are many types of meditation. I have described two different types of mantra meditation practices in The Offer (in the last chapter and in this one). I encourage you to find the type that you personally can connect with the best and the kind that you think that you can practice the most regularly. It is only through a regular and consistent practice that you will get the results from meditation that I describe here.

Chapter 17
Humility

I wanted to write a chapter about a personality characteristic that significantly contributes to long-term heart-centered wealth creation. Humility is necessary for us to answer honestly the question of The Task, who am I? Humility is necessary for me to really admit to myself what it is that I want. Humility is an essential trait necessary to develop empathy. To best engage in community, the ability to exercise humility is essential. Before I point out the speck of dirt in my brother's eye, I need to remove the log from my own. You may have heard this before. Do you know where this saying comes from?

Humility is a tool I need to remedy harm that I may have caused other people in the past. Frequently, our initial responses to stimuli may not be correct. This may be particularly true if you are responding to something that makes you uncomfortable. You may respond to uncomfortable situations, not with your mantra word or with loving-kindness for yourself, but rather with unconscious cognitive biases that you involuntarily deploy to protect yourself.

Your PTSD may be triggered by what are

otherwise unremarkable ordinary events. This is understandable. While my eruption at Lorie was inexcusable, the unprocessed trauma from my divorce had been triggered in me when I emailed her with an unkind message. Humility allowed me to go back and acknowledge my wrongdoing and to at least try to provide restitution to the person I wronged.

My lack of humility manifests in other ways. I told myself for so long that there is no way I could ever be a good public speaker. I am working on developing this skill, but I have let go of this debilitating self-limiting, self-doubting belief first to truly improve. My longtime adherence to this self-limiting belief is important to illustrate how I would rather tell myself lies than act in humility.

My self-limiting belief and cognitive bias were things I had cultivated over a long time. Growing up, I admired people who comfortably could speak naturally in front of a large crowd. I was moved in churches by powerful sermons and admired pastors who genuinely could communicate and illustrate principles from my source text in a relatable way. In my professional life, I was jealous of good public speakers because I knew that it was such a great way to get clients.

Instead of seeking out training or advice or attempting public speaking, I told myself I never could be a good public speaker to protect myself from doing something that I was fundamentally scared to do. I did not want to admit that to myself, though, because I'm a brave, strong, tough, independent person, right? So, I had to retreat to the lie that my natural inclination prevented me from becoming a good public speaker. I set up a lie and then bowed down to it so that I did not have to admit I was a coward. Admitting to cowardice is humiliating.

At some point, I decided to replace this belief. I began to understand some fundamental truths about public speaking. All of humanity is afraid of public speaking and that realization led me to move in the direction of fearlessness, even if I still get nervous before I walk out on a stage. I began to tell myself that public speaking was a skill that I could develop, just like yoga, swimming, playing chess, juggling, poetry, practicing law, all the other skills that I had taken time to develop in my life. To do this, I had to let go of all the thoughts, inhibitions, and self-limiting beliefs that I unwittingly enslaved myself to and that were holding me back from my potential.

You can create an intention to eliminate cognitive biases from your life. I pray that God will reveal mine to me. No matter how painful it may be for me to admit that I am a coward, it still serves me to do so. That is the case because getting past my self-limiting belief and seeking to submit instead to the power of the universe allowed me to trend in the direction of becoming a skilled public speaker. I was never going to accomplish that by thinking it was impossible.

Who do you humble yourself to? Do you pray to the universe that it will guide you in the paths that it thinks you should go in? AS ABOVE, SO BELOW. Do you consider the question of The Task, how can you serve? Or do you enslave yourself (like I do too frequently) to isolating, self-protecting lies that you tell yourself? Do you believe that there is a community of people who love you and have your best interests at heart? When conflict arises, can you exercise sufficient humility to identify the speck in your own eye before blaming the other person for the conflict?

Do you pay attention to your community when you take actions? You will have more success by considering different perspectives than you will by going solely in the direction that you happen to think is right without any reference to anyone around you. Do you have counselors around you, or do you make decisions based solely on the thoughts of your own mind? Do you research matters and submit yourself to knowledge that exists, or do you say that the square wheel is better than the circle? We all fall into self-limiting beliefs and so frequently the reason is that we are too prideful to admit painful truths about ourselves. It may be painful to admit that you are a coward, or that you are ignorant. It may be painful that your cowardice and ignorance, which sometimes were even willful, have led you to conflict in your interpersonal relationships. Having to devote mental and emotional energy to conflict detracts from growth. You may have to admit that you have hurt people in your life as a result of your cognitive biases, and take active humble steps to shed yourself of the negative karma you accumulated in the process. Humility is necessary to take these steps.

    Revealing those painful truths allows you to get in touch with what you really want and who you really are. I had to admit that I was a coward who was willing to lie to protect himself from knowing the truth about his cowardice. How sick is that? It is literal mental illness, but maybe you can identify? As human beings, we can all engage in self-deluding beliefs that look very much like mental illness even if our own circumstances and personal delusions are unique.

Humility can be important as it relates to the concept of mentors. I have had many mentors, but to take full advantage of their input, I had to learn to listen to gain the wisdom that they conveyed. Absorbing knowledge from a mentor frequently requires you to suspend your current way of thinking. This is very difficult for some people. The good news is that meditation and psychedelics can be useful tools to help us move past barriers in our thinking.

Remember me telling you about how MDMA was used to heal PTSD? The people going through this therapy had to humble themselves to the process and the therapists. Remember me telling you about the Ayahuasca ceremony? Everyone going into the ceremony admitted that they were seeking healing from the plant medicine, which was an external source. Everyone was admitting insufficiency and acknowledged a need for help. The beautiful thing that happens in the Ayahuasca ceremony is that when we were all together afterwards, we remained in an emotionally receptive state and we were talking with one another, helping each other process our experiences. We allowed each other to be mentors to one another, and that was enabled by our humility, an acknowledgment that we needed something outside ourselves to thrive. The medicine put us in a receptive mental state so that we could accept common sense input from our community in ways that we could not have before.

Chapter 18

Diet and Wellness

    Real Advisers recommends practical solutions to our clients and attempts to provide relevant information no matter who they may be. An extremely important personal health and wellness upgrade for me was a shift in diet I implemented three years ago. I devote this chapter to information about this dietary change, and other health and wellness recommendations that could benefit everyone including Real Advisers' clients. The health and wellness matters discussed in this chapter can help trend you in the direction of wealth.

    After a weird bout with eczema on my hands and at the recommendation of a nutritionist, in summer 2017 I adopted the keto diet. The keto diet takes advantage of a natural biological process that happens when our bodies enter the fasting, or starvation state. When you begin to starve, your liver produces keto acids that are deployed throughout your body to convert fat stores into glucose for your brain. The keto diet takes advantage of this biological shift and sustains it by limiting carbohydrate intake to less than fifty grams per day. It is important with this diet to consume adequate protein, but the bulk of your calories come from fat. I used to put tablespoons of coconut oil into my smoothies. Now I use bacon fat (instead of vegetable oil) to make my own mayonnaise to go with the hamburger I cook at home, and the to-go pork loin and brisket I get from my favorite fast food barbecue restaurant in Austin, Rudy's. I only eat meat currently on the carnivore diet (a variation of the keto diet).

A result from the keto diet is that you no longer have blood sugar spikes associated with eating sugar (a/k/a carbohydrates) that trigger the insulin response. Your entire source of energy is fat either from dietary or stored sources. You wind up losing a lot of your own fat on the keto diet if you are carrying any excess. As soon as I overcame my psychological and physical addictions to sugar, I began genuinely losing all my desire for the pizza, donuts, and ice cream I used to crave.

The smooth and consistent energy release has increased athletic performance and given me a greater clarity of thought than I experienced before.

In addition, since I am always in a state of starvation (technically), I can easily fast. I can go for extended periods without eating, identifying that the hungry feeling in my stomach frequently is not hunger, but more often thirst. If I can have water, 24-hour fasts are no problem. (I still may drink coffee or tea with my normal Stevia though.) Medical research shows that intermittent fasting is an excellent weight loss tool, and it also has independent health benefits apart from weight loss.

Sugar has been shown to be more physically addictive than cocaine. Along with alcohol, Real Advisers would give you strict warnings against the dangers of sugar, since sugar has been linked to many physical maladies, including obesity, cancer, diabetes, and mental health issues. Disease and unhealth are detractors from wealth accumulation.

Again, none of this is medical or nutritional advice. This is only a description of my personal experience with the keto and carnivore diets I have adopted and adapted to over the past few years. This way of eating has made a dramatic difference in my life. When we give you feedback on your responses to The Task, we will dialogue with you about your diet. Your diet is an important part of your overall health and well-being and healthy people on average are likely to be wealthier.

There is a specific reason for this, and it has to do with the concept of effectiveness. Effectiveness has to do with how efficiently you are deploying energy. You must know who you are, what you want, and where you can serve and then focus your energy in that direction. If you want to achieve your goals, be as efficient as possible with directing your energy toward achieving them.

Use the force multiplier effect mentioned elsewhere in this book. Find other people who are like minded with you. Find people who have similar answers to your questions with The Task. One thing that Real Advisers would like to do is identify similarities among user profiles and connect people with others who are similarly situated to create online communities. These communities could create the real estate investment partnerships described in the horse force multiplier chapter.

Why do I mention this in the same chapter as the chapter about diet and yoga? The reason is because you may be lazy like me, and you may be willing to do more in a community than you would be willing to do alone.

I have experienced the force multiplier effect with group athletic workouts. I work harder at masters swimming than I do when I swim at Barton Springs alone. It is because when I start to get tired but see my friend do a flip turn at the wall to keep going, darn it, if she's going to keep going, then I am too! It is safe for me to manifest an intensified effort because I am working in a group. This is a thing, and you should exploit it everywhere you can in your life. If you want to get in shape, get a coach or do group workouts.

At $88 per month, Black Swan Yoga in Austin is a steal. Before COVID-19, I probably averaged 16-20 classes per month. Let's say I did go to 20 hour-long classes in a month. That is less than $5 per class! Black Swan probably refers me to as a "heavy user", but they certainly appreciate the recurring revenue. They also are donation-based which tells me that Black Swan is a company that is focused on service. Black Swan gives me great value. My teacher, Jennifer Turner, gave me the idea for The Task in a meditation offered in class. Thanks Jenn!

My desire to sit still comfortably for long periods of time has blessed my writing and meditation, so yoga hits me at every level: what I want, who I am, and where I can serve (community). Because my community need is met, I experience the force multiplier effect and have experienced strength gains well into my late 40s. I am thankful for Black Swan and yoga. I am looking forward to returning to in-person classes after COVID-19.

Yoga has been mentioned elsewhere in this book. I cannot recommend the practice of yoga any higher than the practice of meditation as they are intertwined. Yoga is (at least) a breathing and exercise practice designed to condition your body so you can sit still in meditation comfortably for long periods of time. I have experienced the direct benefits of yoga in this way, as fifteen minutes on the floor is no longer uncomfortable for me like it used to be. Yoga is available to people of all ages and I highly encourage it. In fact, my intention is to do a class with one of the Black Swan teachers online tonight through their bsy.tv streaming service.

Finally, what has yoga done but made me more flexible? If I am more flexible, I can better serve my community. There is a worldwide group of people who practice yoga. Wherever you go, you can (at least temporarily) join with that community. Wherever there is community, there is a path to genuine wealth.

The final health and wellness activity that I have only started since my divorce has been ecstatic dance. Ecstatic dance is a thing, and I would encourage you to Google it to watch a video about it to get an idea of what it is like. Think of a drug-free morning time rave, although ecstatic dance itself is what you might see at an ordinary rave. Typically, ecstatic dances are held in the morning or during the day, rather than all night long.

Ecstatic dance was movement therapy for me, and was related to steps I took to meet women after I was divorced. I naturally went to the bars and other locations in Austin where live music is played and where people would dance to music played by DJs. I always noticed that the most beautiful women were on the dance floor so I told myself that that was the place where I needed to be. To do this, I needed to drop all my inhibitions as I had never spent any time in my life on a dance floor until my 40s. I told myself that I would not let my inhibitions get the better of me.

When I first started practicing yoga, I was embarrassed to put my leg up in the air for three-legged dog. Nevertheless, I persisted and overcame my embarrassment to develop a years' long practice that has brought much health and wellbeing to me. We can consciously take actions to force ourselves to overcome inhibitions that are nothing more than cognitive biases. Who cares if people think that I am an idiot for looking goofy on the dance floor, or doing the expected thing of performing unusual postures (*asanas*) at yoga class? I force myself to overcome these inhibitions telling myself that my inhibitions were unreasonable and were preventing me from activities that might bring greater enjoyment and health in my life.

In fact, my friend Agent Red conducts ecstatic dance classes and I attended several of them. She has a method for instructing people about using dance and movement as modes of expression. I would highly recommend her classes just as I would recommend ecstatic dance to you. I would especially recommend it to anybody who like me suffers from inhibitions and sometimes refuses to do things because they are afraid of being embarrassed or believes that they will fail. You can overcome these self-limiting beliefs by focusing your attention on releasing inhibitions. I know this is difficult, but it is well worthwhile.

Chapter 19

Think and Grow Rich

I wanted to devote an entire chapter to Napoleon Hill's book Think and Grow Rich. While its actual connection to Andrew Carnegie may be dubious, there is a reason why Think and Grow Rich has remained so popular since its original publication in 1937. If you do not know specifically what to do now to pursue wealth, or if you are debating whether to read The Offer or TGR first, read Napoleon's book. You can buy mine, but you do not have to read it immediately! Napoleon's is available for free. Do come back to read The Offer because The Offer expands on the principles of TGR.

The central premise of Think and Grow Rich asserts that you can mold your reality according to your thoughts, and this can be used to advance your financial interests.

In similar fashion to The Offer, to implement the principles of TGR, you must determine what it is that you want. TGR provides the following six specific instructions on where to start on your path of wealth accumulation. I quote the entire relevant passage in its entirety:

First. Fix in your mind the exact amount of money you desire. It is not sufficient merely to say "I want plenty of money." Be definite as to the amount. (There is a psychological reason for definite-ness which will be described in a subsequent chapter).

Second. Determine exactly what you intend to give in return for the money you desire. (There is no such reality as "something for nothing.")

Third. Establish a definite date when you intend to possess the money you desire.

Fourth. Create a definite plan for carrying out your desire, and begin at once, whether you are ready or not, to put this plan into action.

Fifth. Write out a clear, concise statement of the amount of money you intend to acquire, name the time limit for its acquisition, state what you intend to give in return for the money, and describe clearly the plan through which you intend to accumulate it.

Sixth. Read your written statement aloud, twice daily, once just before retiring at night, and once after arising in the morning. AS YOU READ, SEE AND FEEL AND BELIEVE YOURSELF ALREADY IN POSSESSION OF THE MONEY.

After reading this in 2017, I wrote out the following:

My Definite Chief Aim, My Major Purpose: to provide for my kids and myself and be a blessing to my world. To glorify God and enjoy him forever.

By January 1, 2027, I will own $10 million and/or enough real estate investments that will generate at least $40,000 in monthly passive income. In return for this money, I will give my full work time and attention as a securities attorney or otherwise. My current plan for accomplishing this is to continue practicing as a securities attorney and taking full advantage of other opportunities that my vocation presents to me. I believe that I will have this money in my possession. My faith is so strong that I can now see this money before my eyes. I can touch it with my hands. It is now awaiting transfer to me at that time, and in the proportion that I deliver the service I intend to render in return for it. I am awaiting a plan by which to accumulate this money, and will follow that plan, when it is received.

In humility, I'm sharing with you what my goal was when I first read TGR and understood its concepts. I also wanted to describe how reading this book is a great first step to wealth creation for anyone, and in fact, reading TGR was my first step on the path that led me to The Offer.

I printed my statement out and tacked it to my wall. At the bottom of the page, I wrote this direct quote from the book:

> "You can never have riches in great quantities UNLESS you can work yourself into a white heat of DESIRE for money, and actually BELIEVE you will possess it."

"The white heat of DESIRE for money" concept challenged me. It sounds like avarice or greed, right?

To answer that, let's pause for a second and ask ourselves what kind of wealth you want to possess? Maybe there is a book out there that you can read that helps you define wealth on your own terms, and provides you with some specific tools to help you achieve that wealth not only for yourself but also for your community? You are reading that very book right now!

You must "actually BELIEVE you will possess" the wealth that I am describing. Your belief about whether you will possess this wealth is informed by how you view the universe.

Do you believe that the universe is arbitrary and mechanistic, devoid of any soul or intention? Alternatively, do I believe that the universe is somehow interconnected, that there is a powerful unseen force out there that is aware of my existence? Do I believe that this awareness includes an actual benevolence toward me and possesses supreme knowledge of every element of my being because somehow, I am part of what it intends for creation? If you have a hard time connecting with this option, this book may not be for you. I will pause, though and mention that for anyone to accumulate great wealth, possess it and enjoy it (wealth=blessing), they must be able to consider things from different perspectives. If you are not wealthy, but only believe in the universe that I described at first (mechanistic), let me suggest that you may need to suspend your view of the universe at least momentarily to become wealthy. Psychedelics help with this and helped me with this immensely.

    This is the case because I really doubted God. I really wondered why a good and loving God would ever allow me to experience the pain of the same tragedy that happened to my parents. I could not imagine why, after vowing never to get a divorce, the same thing happened to me as my parents AND I had four kids. What harm to my children would result from my divorce?

    When I finally started dealing effectively with my childhood trauma and the trauma from my divorce (coincident with my 2012 experiences with psilocybin), I began to perceive genuinely that God was good and that he loved me. Before that time, I always heard that to be true at church, I read it in the Bible, but I never felt it. Then, I get a divorce, the one thing I grew up vowing would never happen to me (particularly if I had kids) because I knew of the pain that it would cause. I knew that from my own experience when my parents divorced when I was five.

    The reason why I am dedicating this book to my mom and dad is because they have taught me more about what it means to be a human being with infinite potential than anyone else. This is the case because they always pointed me in the direction of God. They are my parents, but they also are human beings and I have tried to describe their humanity in these pages. Tolkien wrote about how all our lives are allegories, and my parents have been caring, loving examples of Jesus' love to me. I owe them so much for how they raised me, and even ways that they unintentionally have influenced me.

    Part of the reason my mom and I lived a little isolated from other kids when I was growing up was because my mom had a terrific stay at home job in the 1970s in the women's dormitory at Concordia University in Austin (when it was still on 32nd Street and Interstate 35). My mom and I lived in an apartment within the dorm, and I grew up at Concordia. Remember who I said my friends were? Books! I had access to a small college library growing up. I had an internet equivalent in the 1970s and back then we called them libraries. This library was readily available to me when most kids my age only (maybe) had a local public library within walking distance of their home. None of them likely had ready access to the library of the caliber that I did. I was the wealthiest kid in Austin, and I didn't even know it. My fabulous wealth was so ordinary I couldn't recognize it for what it was at the time.

After writing this, I realized that I truly am the wealthiest man in the universe, because no one defines wealth just like me and I have the key to how I can become wealthy. I already am wealthy and I am going to continue in my life on the path I am describing here to accumulate more and more wealth. It is an inevitability.

This is the secret of wealth. When I look deep into my source text, I understand that it instructs me that my fundamental purpose is to enjoy life. This includes a deep consideration of the questions, who am I and what do I want? My enjoyment is determined by reference to what I want and who I am. This is true not only for me but for EVERYONE. I am informed that enjoyment must be connected to the notion of service, or put another way, to the notion of love. Our service toward one another, and loving one another, occurs in community.

    I had no idea in 2017 when I wrote my TGR statement how all the things I describe in this book might come about. Immediately after I wrote my statement, in addition to working hard at my law practice (my highest hourly rate), I internally committed to the course of continuing to write the T. H. Chalm Bible poetry I described. I started with Psalms, then worked on Job, and finally, I finished Rhyming Solomon, including Song of Songs, Proverbs, and Ecclesiastes. I had no other idea about what I wanted to write about, but I knew that this project would be a way for me to worship my source and learn more about my source's characteristics. Also, I knew that by defining such specific parameters for my writing (rhyming iambic pentameter), writing this poetry would be like a gym for my writing skills. I can say that my writing skills improved tremendously with the Bible poetry I've written. You may not enjoy it, but The Offer poem is very representative of my Bible poetry and includes lines from Ecclesiastes. I love the jarring and unusual syntax that results from reordering words to conform to the meter. I think that this promotes thought, and if you go through and read one of my poems, it may cause you to see the Bible in a different way.

I even imagined that a Satanist could read my poetry and say this, "I hate this because it's about Jesus, but it's not bad poetry." If I accomplished that, it would be an evangelical outreach success through art! My religion says that I should share the Gospel (the good news about Jesus), but that is a thing because we are supposed to believe that the Gospel is good news. Later chapters in this book provide some observations about modern American Christianity, particularly as the Gospel is preached as a means toward getting rich (without a corresponding discussion of the matters described herein).

Through my poetry, I was refining my craft as a creative writer. Little did I knew that my source was using this exercise to train me as a writer for another genre of literature, and this training allowed me to write the core of The Offer (around 150 pages) in a matter of about four days. I have a "white heat of DESIRE" for

The Offer.

Did you see anything in my TGR statement about poetry? I was still so out of touch with my identity that I did not even include anything about creative writing in my statement. To be fair to myself, I had a vague notion about how, if I had more money, I could have more time to devote to activities that I loved. Knowing that I loved to write poetry, having more money might give me more time to write.

My writing incorporated a notion about community because part of my ambition with writing is to write books that sell millions of copies, right? I am pretty smart and have a lot of really good ideas, and I've read and digested A LOT of really good information. Through The Offer, I discovered that I at least had the potential to write something that people might be able to connect with more than my poetry.

I always had a dream of wanting to bless people through my writing, just like I was blessed as a lonely child whose best friends were books. My writing is my attempt to rescue that child who exists out there now in someone else. There are other people in the world who are lonely, who feel as if they do not have any help, and I thought that at the very least, maybe I could just write a letter encouraging them.

Writing was my highest calling ever since I started reading Narnia when I was around eight years old, and then LOTR when I was ten. Aragorn and Aslan were my ideal men and I identified with them strongly. (I prefer Aragorn, though, because it is easier for me to identify with a man than a lion.) They were my mentors, and those books provided me with solace. I cultivated my imagination by exploring both Narnia and Middle Earth in my mind. This is why writing is such a core part of my identity because I am desperately trying to reach that lonely child with some words that may bring him comfort even though he has no one else to encourage him.

I am writing to all the actually poor people, or the poor in spirit, and want to encourage them to humility (meekness) because my source tells me that the meek inherit the earth. Do you want to be wealthy like I define it in this book? Do you want to be wealthy like the wealthiest man in history defined *true* wealth?

Notice, that immediately after I wrote my statement in 2017, my eruption at Lorie occurred, and as a result, I resigned from a good professional opportunity in shame. Because of my unprocessed trauma, I sabotaged myself.

The beautiful thing about this story, though, is that immediately after my unprofessional email and resignation from Adventum, a *bodhisattva* appeared to challenge me about meditation.

I did not know how I was going to achieve the wealth that The Offer represents to me. Nevertheless, Solomon, through his wisdom and my work on the Chalm poetry with Ecclesiastes specifically led me here, now, to both register Real Advisers as an investment adviser and write The Offer.

At the very moment The Offer was created I realized with greater specificity what it was that I wanted to do. Remember what I said about how I have a present ambition that sounds a little preposterous? My present ambition is to go back to school on a full-time basis as a 49-year-old man and pursue a Master of Fine Arts in poetry. I don't know if that is the place where I can best serve, and I have asked for advice from people in my community (including some of the smartest, wealthiest, and most highly-regarded attorneys and other business people in Austin) about whether I should do this. They will have to pay me to do it so they will need to think about this question for a while.

In humility, I will accept their answer, knowing that it may be in their best interests for me to keep writing. That is the case if The Offer is a legitimate way to promote an investment advisory business. I wrote the core of this book in about a week, and the way that the ideas keep flowing, and how much I know it resonates with everyone that I describe it to (except for the curmudgeons, and I try not to spend too much time with them), I think there is a great deal of additional intellectual property that can be created with The Offer. It may be in Real Advisers' best interests to fund my writing. I will ask them for permission to devote time to getting an MFA, but the main thing for me will be to continue to engage with the core of my identity, my passion to be a creative writer.

I know that I will be exercising this passion for the rest of my life. I can continue to exercise my passion for writing as a practicing attorney. I could be exercising another secret ambition that I have denied myself through the same lie I told myself about not being creative enough; this secret ambition is to write science fiction. I could write more Bible poetry. I could write for Real Advisers. I joke with Jon that he and I will be happy in the nursing home because we can play chess, and when I get tired of that I can write poetry. Writing is such a fundamental part of my identity because every time I craft a sentence or express a thought, I am engaging in a process that helps me reach the lonely 10-year-old Roland. When he looked for a friend, he found solace in books and maybe I can write some cool science fiction story that will be a gift to kids in the future. Who knows? AS ABOVE, SO BELOW.

The beautiful thing about The Offer is that it should reconnect you with your identity. I told a friend last night that my 17-year-old self would look at me now, at 49 and give me a fist bump. He would be disappointed about how unkindly I have acted toward people in my life (particularly Aricka) but at least he would see that we survived the depression, anxiety, and endless successions of suicidal ideations we lived with for years. He would see that at age 49, we are thriving despite my failures, and in fact, we're peaking in our overall experience. Life has never been better for me than right now.

The universe carried me along despite my failures and enabled its intention to bring me to a place of genuine wealth. My 17-year-old self would be pleased with me. I know this because I am pleased with myself and I say that without pride. Everyone should be able to say that genuinely and without arrogance. It is possible to say that in humility because we can only be truly pleased with ourselves if we are serving.

Ecclesiastes directed me to a path of wealth. All I did was ask my three questions. I started to answer those questions immediately after I heard them in yoga class from Jenn. This is a perfect illustration of the notion of community and how I was blessed through my community, by hearing other ideas besides my own. By exercising humility and actually listening to what Jenn said, she revealed a perspective that I did not have. To hear what she was saying, I had to tell myself that even though I am super intelligent and have a lot of valuable information in my head, other people STILL can communicate valuable information to me!

As my wealth began to grow, not only in my bank account but also in my mind and in my community, I began to be more authentic and genuine with people. My empathy expanded and I was able to be more attentive with my friends. I could more easily tolerate temporary misunderstandings where in the past I would write people off at the most minor of offenses. In the past I was unable to circle back around with people and tell them that even though we are in a disagreement (we have these diametrically opposed perspectives and it seems like they both can't be "true" at the same time), I would still like to be your friend. Meditation has allowed me to sit with uncomfortable silences and simply think (rather than react) in those instances where my friends seem to have an opposite way of viewing shared circumstances. I remain present at these times even when the opposing perspectives seems to be at odds with our friendship.

    For the sake of relationships, out of a spirit of humility, and because we want to continue to experience the force multiplier effect of communities that I describe elsewhere, we may want to overlook minor slights. We may want to acknowledge how we ourselves may frequently make mistakes. We should never make the mistake of impairing relationships that enable valuable force multiplier effects in our lives. This is particularly the case if these people are part of your community. This is even more particularly the case if these people are part of your faith-based community. We must be prepared to exercise humility with each other to maintain the efficiencies and effectiveness necessary for the creation of the true wealth I describe in The Offer.

My teacher (Rabbi) instructed me that we should love one another. This is a simple way of saying that we must be gentle with other people and it probably is in our personal best interest to extend more grace toward people than we do at present.

Do you see what can happen when you follow these principles and the ideas in TGR? I didn't even finish reading Think and Grow Rich. Napoleon Hill writes in its first chapters that as soon as you understand its central premise, that your thoughts create your own reality, you can quit reading. I told you that about The Offer back in Chapter 1, didn't I? When I understood TGR and its consistency with my core belief system, I stopped reading and started writing. I proceeded on with my life and the things happened that I described to you here.

The Offer is the universe's invitation to you to step into abundance. Please join me on a path of creating great wealth based on the principles of The Offer.

Chapter 20

Education and the Scope of Ambition/Service

When Darrell Windham began describing his passion for the affordability of American public education, I immediately understood his rationale. Darrell is a little older than me, but we both attended the University of Texas at Austin for our undergraduate degrees. He went there for law school, and neither of us ever paid more than about $2,000 per semester in tuition. That person was me when I was an undergraduate student, and I graduated with my bachelor's degree in 1994. Darrell told me that he paid less than $500 per semester for LAW SCHOOL! UT is a great law school, and I could not get admitted there despite applying twice. I went to Southern Methodist University School of Law in Dallas (another great law school in Texas!).

I want you to know who Darrell Windham is to me and why he has been my most important professional mentor. In 2000, Darrell hired me to be an apprentice attorney when he was a shareholder and head of the corporate and securities law practice group at Winstead, a Texas law firm whose eponymous attorney (Pete) officed in Austin. I had been out of law school for about two years. Darrell Windham, Paul Tobias, and Richard

Ressler taught me securities law (which must be learned in a very hands-on way), but Darrell informed my life uniquely. He continues to do so, and I am so grateful for my friendship with him.

Darrell and I both came from similar economic backgrounds. He told me about being raised by loving parents, but also about his father having to work multiple jobs to make ends meet for his family. Despite our humble economic circumstances, Darrell and I both were blessed to be able to obtain our college and post-graduate educations at a time when it was much more affordable to do so than now.

Darrell's concern about funding for American public university-level education is understandable. Undergraduate (and graduate) tuition rates have exploded during the last 30 years, even in public universities. This has been reported widely. These increasing costs significantly change the value proposition of education for people like me who know that the best investment decision I ever made was to borrow the money I needed for my law degree. That going to law school for Darrel and me was a great investment decision is certainly true if you pay the tuitions that we did. My tuition at SMU in the late 1990s was around $35,000 per year. I took out loans and Aricka worked at SMU while we were married, so I got a discount. It was still expensive, but I ended school with only about $125,000 in student loans.

That still was the best investment I ever made, but what if that amount had been $350,000 instead? It becomes a different value proposition. To make my investment decision as a 25-year-old, it was impossible for me to see with certainty whether I would get my expected payout. I took the same blind leap of faith that many young people do and told myself that I was going to risk it. I told myself that I had to try because this was my vision, and there was a way (student loans) that could enable me as a poor kid to go to law school. By going to law school, I was seeking to improve my economic status.

Is that still available to the kid who must take out $350,000 in loans instead? That is a MUCH bigger leap of faith. If you are going to law school now, I would really encourage you to study computer science to think about how computers will be used to perform many of the functions that attorneys currently do. We will all be replaced by robots in our jobs someday (and maybe very soon), so make sure you analyze how you will continue to make money when the robots come for your job. You can program the robot and the only people who will be able to program the lawyer robots are attorneys who know what it means to practice law. You will need to learn that AND how to program the robot at the same time.

If you are wanting to be a creative writer, I would not recommend taking out a $350,000 loan for your education unless you have written a best seller that sold millions of copies. Then the student loan *may* be the very best way to finance an MFA because there may be student loan forgiveness in the future with a change in the way our federal government is run. Who knows?

I was blessed by entering a career (law) with high income potential. It has high income potential because attorneys can earn such high hourly rates. When you are in a place where you are having to work for others, try to maximize your hourly rate. More money, more time, right? All things being equal, maximizing your hourly rate will trend you in the direction of wealth.

Note that the only reason that I am able to express all of this is that somehow all my ambition, intelligence, desire for monetary wealth, desire to be a writer, and also my deceptive self-denials drove me here.

I accomplished the goal I had when I dreamed of being a creative writer as a teenager despite myself.

Education was essential to the fulfillment of my goals. Education is necessary for anyone to fulfill their goals. It is a thing. Whatever dream anyone is pursuing, they should at least consider that there are people who went before them pursuing similar dreams in the past. These people may have left behind them written information that could inform the present about the best and most efficient means and manners to pursue goals. Analyzing this information is education. You inevitably will come up with your own original ways and methods, but it is arrogant, inefficient, and a failure to exercise humility to think that you cannot learn from the people that went before you. It is foolishness.

Without being able to engage in the exercise of education, though, we will be left with an uneducated workforce. I told Darrell that I wanted to give millions of dollars to whatever charitable organizations are working to either fund public education in the United States, or taking steps to somehow remedy its tragic overpricing. These are giving targets for Real Advisers because we want to help people at every level. We want to help the entire country to heal trauma and develop an educated workforce. If we do not do this, we will not continue to be as competitive with the world as we have in the past. The rest of the world has a hunger to take their places at the top of the heap that the United States has occupied for so long.

Everything I describe in this book will help to strengthen yourself and your communities and make you wealthier. Your communities built on top of each other constitute larger political subdivisions. All of us coming together in the states make up an entire nation, the United States. I am not a nationalist, but I do believe that there remain principles that are expressed in the United States' charter documents that everyone believes in. Most people believe at some level that the tenets of the Declaration of Independence, the Constitution and the Bill of Rights form a good basis for government, even if they can use some improvement. (We can never forget or condone the Constitution's concessions to the enslavement of people of African descent, for instance.)

Personally, before the United States can move forward in a heart-centered way, we should acknowledge to ourselves that we are a nation founded on human trafficking. The negative effects of this national intergenerational trauma persist today. We must acknowledge the ugliness of slavery and how all our society is built upon or somehow influenced by that fundamental moral and economic degradation of humanity that occurred in United States prior to the Civil War. That degradation continues now with systemic racism. Real Advisers wants to work against systemic racism.

There is another reason why education is so important to The Offer. Remember I said I wanted to write science fiction? In my recent daydream I asked, why build a rocket ship that can go to Mars if your intent is only to go to the moon? This relates to the notion of both ambition and service because here again, as with the hourly rate, people tend to de-value themselves. Because of past degradation, trauma, a lack of imagination, or a lack of information, people struggle to conceive of how valuable they are intrinsically. Education is so important because education informs you about possibilities. I learned about so many possibilities in everything that I studied, even if the things I learned about were not directly related to my eventual profession. I was exposed to new ideas and those new ideas allowed me to expand my ambitions. Not only have my ambitions served my own interests (when exercised in a healthy way) but they better serve the interests of my community.

If our potential is limitless, then we should build not only interstellar, but interdimensional rocket ships. So I can know what is possible for myself and possible for my community, I must educate myself about possibilities. I must not allow myself to ever persist in ignorance when the information that could benefit me and my community is so readily available.

The information I just described is becoming both more and less readily available. The proliferation of information through the Internet and the rising costs of American college have occurred simultaneously. While information is imminently available, we all can appreciate how training is needed to parse through the abundant information to assess its provenance. School taught by learned professors is a thing and it is necessary. Nevertheless, a young person may become so discouraged by the looming cost of a degree that they decide to give up on their dreams. When this happens, it is tragedy because of the infinite potential all humans share.

Chapter 21
Enjoy Your Toil--Acceptance

I would rather not dwell too much on the portion of Ecclesiastes that discusses enjoying your toil. Enjoying toil sounds sadistic or masochistic, right? I would like to challenge that notion, particularly by reference to the story I told you about my dad, and how he feels wealthy in his truck driving to the baseball games that he umpires. This would be drudgery and toil to me, but because my dad has ingeniously combined his rest (something he enjoys) with industry, he experiences effortless enjoyment of his "toil".

Many people think about toil and feel the same way I do, that it sounds like pushing a rock up a mountain only to see it fall down again on the other side the next day. The 20th century French existential philosopher Albert Camus employed the ancient Greek myth of Sisyphus to demonstrate that we should live our lives even in the face of the absurdity of our uselessness, knowing that no matter our efforts or virtue in this world, in the end we all will die. We can get depressed about that and become suicidal like I did, or we can accept the fundamental absurdity of this notion and revel in it. Camus gives some valuable recommendations, and

I would recommend his book, The Myth of Sisyphus highly.

One thing worth noting here specifically is that community can provide deep meaning. Even if you do not believe in an immortal existence, you at least can acknowledge that there will be people in the world who will live after you. You could say that you do not care because after you're dead you will have no further knowledge of the affairs of the living. Do you not have anyone to love in the world? A person that loves no one is pitiable and must be miserable.

I mentioned before how in 2017 I was directed on a path that did not seem at all related to my goal of accumulating $10 million. I perceived that my poetry was not very popular. I knew quickly that I would never get rich by selling it, but I didn't care. I really liked what I was writing and found it gratifying. I felt like for the first time I understood many of the scriptures that previously just danced through and read quickly without comprehending their depths. I don't say this to assert the truth of my sacred text or to persuade you to become a Christian (although if you want to I will talk with you about that), but only as an example of how, when I asked the universe for something, the universe drew me to itself. The universe said, "Know more about me before you get to a place of thinking about yourself." Of course, the universe knew that when I hit Solomon's words in Ecclesiastes, I would have the gift of true wealth as described in The Offer:

> To all whom God gives both possessions wealth,
> and likewise, whom he has enabled well,
> to find enjoyment, to accept their lot
> in all their toils this is the gift of God.

This is where the universe left me after I prayed for my reward. When I was writing the poetry, at times I got discouraged. Nevertheless, I also was so inspired because I knew of the great potential of what I was writing. What if my poetry could draw other people to my source text like it did with me? At the very least I knew that my mom and dad both liked it. Even as a 49-year-old man they could take pleasure in their son exercising his creative talents just like you can with your five-year-old son drawing pictures with crayons at the kitchen table. There is nothing wrong with being proud of your five-year-old son, and there's nothing wrong with being proud of your 49-year-old son. Your 49-year-old son, though, knows how to analyze and determine whether that poetry is just something that his mom and dad might enjoy or maybe it is something that the whole world would enjoy.

    I have received enough positive feedback from people other than my mom and dad to make me believe that my Bible poetry is a blessing, and thus, it may be worthwhile for me to continue to write. Consequently, I continue to write it and I currently am about halfway through Isaiah. I stay true to my focus writing under the name of a pseudonym and writing poetry that over the last few years I do not think many people have read. That is okay because I was doing it for myself trying to train myself to write better. I knew that I would write this poetry and it would teach me how to be a better writer. I knew that somehow the universe would use that skill for other purposes, or maybe it wouldn't. Maybe I could just use this skill for the sole purpose of my enjoyment, my pleasure! I continued to adhere to the process and eventually after three years of writing only Bible poetry, in 2020, The Offer came to me. I wrote it very quickly and with a great amount of clarity, desire, intention, and passion.

    One of my favorites artists in Austin is a painter and creator of collages named Spencer Smith. We were talking recently at Jon's art gallery where Spencer's work was displayed. He described how he had completed a large body of work because of COVID-19. He said that in this sense COVID-19 drove him to work harder and he produced more art. I told him I identified with that myself.

When I got my direction to write those five or six Bible poetry books, I did not understand how that related to me accumulating $10 million dollars of real estate. Nevertheless, the poetry was the direction that the universe put me on and I was at peace because I was really enjoying the project. I knew that my writing was improving. I would read back over things that I wrote with pride and have that sense that many artists share, that in my poetry, the universe was communicating through me and allowing me to transmit ideas that I never could have come up with on my own. What a gift and blessing! I felt like the voice of the universe sometimes. That is agency.

My friend Spencer spends his time working at a job that involves driving a truck. He paints and creates collages in all his spare time when he is not working. I can identify with this. I practice the law in all my working hours, and I devote as much as myself as I can to my poetry when I am not attending to my legal practice. Many times, I would much rather write poetry than practice law. I can gain acceptance by remembering that the work that I do practicing law influences my poetry, and of course the same is true in reverse. My law career has been a fantastic blessing to me. It has allowed me to make a decent living, but it also has made me into a better poet simply because I am a better writer for having practiced law. Being a writer and learning how to write as an attorney is a thing! I tell people now that I am a writer instead of a lawyer, and they are intrigued rather than impressed. I would much rather cultivate love than fear in my life.

    Spencer is a collage artist, and, in his art, he takes related but disparate images and combines them into a unified single image that has special relevance and artistic meaning. I told Spencer that he should never feel discouraged driving the truck because he is absorbing so much source material in the world, seeing so much more of it than I ever do. I typically drive around in the same routes every day: back and forth to my office; the grocery store; my favorite barbecue store; back and forth from Jon's apartment (where Spencer has a studio) to play chess; back and forth to be with my kids. I run in the same grooves all the time. Spencer goes to random locations and absorbs all the images that he sees on his way. I know that he uses what he absorbs from the world in his art.

Neither Spencer nor I are earning a living from our art (yet). We both are wealthy men in our art, though, because we engage in our art even while acknowledging that we are working on things that seemingly do not have direct apparent significance or relevance. Nevertheless, we know that we are refining and focusing our craft and so in that sense, our work is always being rewarded.

I wanted to mention an excellent quote from the 2nd century BCE holy book of the Hindu faith, the Bhagavad Gita. I must confess that I only know about this quote because I read it in B. K. S Iyengar's excellent Light on Yoga. The passage is a few lines long but well worth quoting in its entirety:

> Work alone is your privilege, never the fruits thereof. Never let the fruits of action be your motive; and never cease to work. Work in the name of the Lord, abandoning selfish desires. Be not affected by success or failure. This equipoise is called Yoga.

This passage speaks to me much about the notion of acceptance, finding joy in toil, and yoga. This passage is highly relevant for The Offer.

    Spencer's art is really cool. In fact, last night I just bought another one of his prints for $300. I love his art because it combines images of pop culture and it is psychedelically inspired. It is intentionally subversive as all good art should be and Spencer is a direct artistic descendant of Andy Warhol. We all know how popular he was. I do not know whether Spencer's works will ever sell for millions like Andy's, but Spencer has that potential. Why? Because Spencer, just like you and me, has infinite value!

    Spencer satisfies the definition of wealth because he accepts his toil as a delivery driver and finds joy in it. He agrees with me about how much more of popular culture he absorbs because of his job, and it comes out in cool and weird ways in his art. I know of the joy that he feels when he produces his art and when he is in his community since I'm part of his community.

    Spencer is young but also feels the urgency of how his time may be wasted because of the energy he devotes to his "day" job. This is the case because his higher calling probably is the painting. He is simply so skilled with his art, and in fact, art may be where he earns his highest hourly rate. All things being equal, if you are working for other people, try to move yourself in the direction of maximizing your hourly rate because this will lead to more money and more time.

    I cannot imagine that the universe gave Spencer the gifts he possesses not wanting them to be on full display through his art. His art challenges our sensibilities and I joked last night with him and Jon that Spencer's art makes me feel "uncomfortable". They laughed.

    My whole point of this chapter is to let you know that you may be working on something right now that does not seem like it is directing you towards your goals. I deeply understand that and all I can do is encourage you to persist as I mentioned in Chapter 19 about Think and Grow Rich. If you do not know what to do at this very moment to better achieve your goals, the best things you can do are begin a regular meditation practice, start practicing yoga, and read Think and Grow Rich. The cool thing about that book is that you really do have to just read the first chapter until Napoleon says you can stop reading once you understand its premise. I wrote down my chief aim and goal and waited. I cannot guarantee that you're going to become a millionaire but if you adopt the principles in TGR and The Offer, I know that you can become wealthy by the definition of wealth that we've been describing here. Don't forget: you define wealth for yourself, according to your personal values.

Chapter 22
Bobby McGee and Freedom

Janis Joplin sings about freedom being just another word for having nothing left to lose. This is a thing. If you find yourself in a place where you never have any money and the bills always seem to overwhelm, I know that the message of acceptance in the last chapter is difficult. I nevertheless would not be honest if I failed to note that your humble state in life may afford you freedoms that wealthy people lack.

I have a very wealthy friend, and let's call him Joaquin because my friend values his privacy. Joaquin manages his family's wealth, but he still is answerable to a board of trustees from whom he is duty bound to take direction. I perceive that Joaquin's behavior in life is somewhat restricted. He told me how his board pays attention to things he does and how he represents their family's interests in his day-to-day life. In some ways, his life may be scrutinized like the life of a member of the British royal family. As a middle-aged man now, he has more freedoms, and they understand that he is a human being. It seems like he has a great deal of freedom of expression generally. Let's also say that Joaquin is one of the most respected medical professionals in his field. His family can hold him up in a place of great honor because he has demonstrated professional excellence (outside of his family's wealth) that is undeniable by the world.

Joaquin bears his responsibilities admirably. I know that he feels the weight of his responsibilities and sometimes wishes that he could simply unburden himself because he gets tired just like you and me. I know Joaquin listens to and obeys his family members in humility. It is an amazing thing to hear him talk about this relationship because it is incomparable with most people's ordinary experience. Joaquin's role is not different from the president of a corporation being answerable to his board of trustees. The board of directors for sure might fire the president, but I don't know anything about the termination provisions related to Joaquin's position, whether he can be fired or resign. It is a mystery to me and I do not pry into his affairs.

Joaquin must manage his family's wealth not only for himself but also for their benefit (and with their help, advice, and supervision). Consequently, they must inform him of how they perceive his life affecting his responsibilities to manage the wealth and make decisions about how it should be deployed. This is Joaquin's community. He is deeply ingrained in this community, he serves his community, and they serve him as well. His community is a central focus of his life and identity, and again, Joaquin is a person whom I would describe as truly wealthy by any measure. Because I know him personally, I know that Joaquin knows how to enjoy his life. He's a wealthy man despite his bank account (of which I have no specific knowledge), but his freedom is constrained because of his family's oversight of his life.

If you have limited resources, think about this. Lawsuits in business are common but no one will ever bring a lawsuit against you if they do not think that they can recover on a judgment. A poor defendant is not a good defendant. We can possibly identify with The Notorious B.I.G.'s assertion that

> I don't know what they want from me
> It's like the more money we come across
> The more problems we see

If you are asking for more money, then anticipate more problems. I am not discouraging you from asking for more money but make sure that you're developing skills that allow you to deal with problems. Here again I emphasize that you should meditate. Meditation can be used as a tool to calm yourselves in moments of high anxiety where you are trying to come up with solutions for problems. The solutions may be revealed to you over time or from the counsel of your community. If you ever are uncertain about how to act, the best thing that you can do is wait and meditate and look inside yourself. The goal is to answer the questions of The Task. Ask for more money, but simultaneously consider Solomon's prayer to God. Before he asked for riches, he asked God for wisdom. God told Solomon that because he asked for wisdom before wealth, God would give him both as a reward.

When I was young and wanted money, I prayed the same prayer thinking that I had found the loophole. I didn't ask God for money since I doubted his goodness. Because he probably wasn't good, he would never give me what I wanted. I attempted to deceive God suggesting to him that my sole desire was for wisdom. Do you think he knew the truth? Do you think the universe enables its intentions?

Solomon is described in the Bible as the most fabulously wealthy man in history. I love Ecclesiastes, written by Solomon, for the reasons I've described so far, but also because of the words that he writes about how "everything is meaningless" and that all we can do "under the sun" is enjoy our life and give Glory to God. Remember how I described the Westminster confession?

Solomon was connected with the myth of Sisyphus in the sense that he recognized the absurdity of our actions and efforts, and meaninglessness of everything that we do here in this life because it all ends in our deaths. Yet he said that the best thing we can do is enjoy our lives. That's the central premise of The Offer.

This challenges many people's notion that they need to be productive in their lives. That is probably true because we all must eat, and we all might have somebody in our lives that we're responsible for feeding (at least for a short time). Also, it is true at least to a degree that our personal productivity is related to how we can best serve. What was hardest for me to think about was the concept of rest and the necessity for rest in order to work hard. I was very challenged by the notion that my sole purpose in life is to enjoy it.

I am a *Streber*, a gunner, a try hard. In German, it is not a complimentary term. It describes a prideful person who always thinks that he can achieve everything through his own actions. He grates on people's nerves because all he can think and talk about is how he is ambitious and how he will achieve everything. We all know people like this. I have been that person and I still am to a large degree. The most important thing I had to learn was the notion of rest and trusting in process. Acceptance was a difficult lesson for me, and it is for most people.

We should never forget our essentially free natures. I know that Joaquin does not feel so constrained by his family that he is completely unable to express himself. He accepts the minor limitations they may express towards him and he moves forward in the confidence that at the heart of his community, centered around his family, are the ideas of love and service.

Take advantage of the time when you may be poor to explore all the possibilities. This is a time where you are not confronted with the types of problems that are associated with wealth: how to invest it; and how to make sure that other people may be blessed through your wealth. Begin to contemplate these principles so that you can go on and create wealth for yourself and your community.

A great tragedy occurs when someone becomes wealthy, but they do not know how to use their newfound wealth responsibly. This circumstance is best illustrated by the lottery winner who is bankrupt after a year of profligate spending and succumbing to solicitations for cash from friends and family.

Meditation is a tool that can bring you rest even in those moments when you are at your most economically challenged. I understand those challenges and I want to have compassion. There are many people who may be reading this that I will never be able to help other than with my words. I hope that somehow you will be driven to your source of creation, your source texts, or other philosophical works like Camus', all of which can provide hope for people who are discouraged or even suicidal.

As a wealth advisor, I would commend gratitude to you. Even at our poorest moments financially, we frequently still can find things to be grateful for. Cultivating gratitude can be a key factor in developing life satisfaction, but gratitude requires mental discipline just like turning away from anger.

As a wealth advisor, I would commend to all my clients those things in life that provide deep meaning but that are FREE. In my life, poetry costs me only the expense of a pen and paper. Meditation is free. Yoga is nearly. Ecstatic dances are inexpensive to attend, but sometimes, I dance to music in my kitchen, another free activity. A walk in your neighborhood, a conversation with a friend, a game of chess, the joy of participating in a community activity all are things that you can do to improve your life condition, and all these things are free or nearly free. I also understand that growing cannabis and mushrooms is relatively simple and inexpensive, and can be done indoors, even in closets. Check out your local library. There are abundant reading and educational materials available for checkout for free. (Of course, the internet is a bottomless well of "free" information, some of which is valuable.) Enriching your mind makes you wealthier by any measure and prepares you for when you will have greater material wealth in the future.

    The main takeaway from this chapter is that even though you are poor, think about your blessings of freedom. Please know that I would never commend freedom to someone who is homeless or hungry. The only good news for people in those conditions is that they may be at their extreme low point, and many people identify their bottom as the place where they finally were able to begin making true change. I identify with this.

Last, there is a relationship between the cultivation of freedom and rest. When we are at rest, we are free from our burdens. When we are on vacation, we are not working. For me freedom means rest. Consequently, connecting myself to the notion of freedom has allowed me to rest better, and further, to work harder. That is a blessing to me, because I confess, I can be lazy.

Chapter 23

Modern American Christianity—Part 1

I would only recommend that you read this chapter and the next if you are a Christian or are curious about Christianity. I only include these chapters in The Offer because I want to improve my faith-based community, Christianity. Christianity's relevance in modern American culture is in severe decline. Consequently, Christianity in the United States needs reformation. Following the suggestions included in these two chapters could help make the church more relevant as it reflects to a greater degree the unconditional love of Jesus. It is only through that love that Jesus and the Gospel will be relevant to anybody in the 21st Century.

First, there exists an ugly strain of American Christianity that proposes that Jesus will make you wealthy if you ask him. The prosperity gospel can lead people to believe that if you are not rich and a Christian, there is something wrong with your life. Somehow you are sinful if you are poor.

I suppose you could say sin is unprocessed trauma, and maybe this association between unrighteousness and poverty would be correct in a way.

It would heartless in the extreme, however, to think this because people suffering from trauma almost always are victims. Further, the problem is that the prosperity gospel usually is interpreted as a belief that the rich are blessed, but the poor are cursed sinners. This ignores some underlying egalitarian principles of my faith that assert that there was only ever one perfect man, and we all are equally imperfect in the sense that God looks on us all the same. Maybe you are richer than me (your bank account is bigger) but we will all face a shared trauma. Our mortality is the equalizing fact of humanity.

  I want to be very clear that I am not promoting the real Gospel in The Offer as a means to acquire wealth, defined strictly as dollars in your bank account. What I am saying here is that the Gospel (that incorporates both Christianity and Judaism) agrees with The Bible Study. The Bible Study is directly from the Bible, from the Book of Ecclesiastes. I know there are fine details where we may disagree, but please let me know if you can find fault in The Bible Study that prevents your acceptance or understanding of The Offer. I believe that we can all use The Offer as a model for creating real heart-centered wealth. This is regardless of your specific belief system. This is the case because true wealth equals enjoyment, and that is something with which all of humanity can identify. Also, it is hard to argue that wealth can be enjoyed apart from community.

American Christianity seems to lack sensitivity about how the world perceives the church as a representative and enforcer of the patriarchy. People perceive Christianity and the church as a force that only strengthens systemic abuses of power and shaming power structures that are used to subjugate people of color, women, children, and people from the LGBT community. The example of the Catholic church cannot be ignored, particularly by people traumatized by their crimes. The rape of children is one of the most horrific crimes only exceeded by murder. I hate to say it, but the church has enabled child rape. That is an ugly thing to say about my religion.

It is somewhat ironic that the church exercises so much discrimination against marginalized groups because I believe that the increased egalitarianism that we see in our culture generally (despite the continuing systemic racism, sexism, and hate) is a direct result of the permeation of the Gospel through our world during the last two millennia. I say this despite all the evils that have been done in the name of Jesus by his followers. This is an idea I should fully flesh out in another book.

My point is to admonish my fellow Christians that we live in a postmodern American society where we should be extraordinarily sensitive to how we are perceived as Christians. To be true evangelists, we should follow some of Jesus' instructions about binding up wounds, healing the sick, and providing for the poor before we tell people that they are going to hell because they are gay.

Jesus gave his gift of love to the world unconditionally and the church will only connect with the world if it reflects that same unconditional love. Who are we to put ourselves in a place of authority over Jesus? How can we as mere humans ever seek to qualify his divine love? While I am very skeptical of how my religion is practiced, I continue to engage in my faith. Jesus embodies an essential message of love and forgiveness that transcends the evils done by the church. Despite the evils done in Jesus name, I still believe in him and want to engage in the practice of my religion.

I encourage you to engage in your religion and engage in your faith. Engaging in your faith is an important component of wellness and health. Your faith tradition probably includes a branch that emphasizes meditation. Almost all faiths have engaged with meditation. It is a thing with all religions, at least in one of their various iterations, denominations, or sects, including Christianity. Ironically, this is untrue with modern Christianity in the United States. While the church in the United States certainly advocates prayer (petitioning the deity) and worship, they look askance at meditation and yoga as Eastern Occultic practices and evidence that you are invoking foreign gods.

There are reasons to protect Christian brothers from harm. I may have the liberty (freedom) to do certain things, like eat meat sacrificed to idols (as referred to in 1 Corinthians 8) that other weaker brothers' consciences do not allow. So, to love them and shield them like children, I should make sure that they always fully understand the intentions behind my actions. That is why I give such explicit instructions about yoga and meditation because this book is a book that is written to Christians. It also is written to everyone because the principles described here can help everyone regardless of their beliefs.

The best response to Christian skeptics of yoga and meditation is to ask them what they think

Christianity is? Is it not in fact an Eastern occultic religion itself, and if it is not, please tell me what you think it is? If it disturbs you to think of Christianity as occultic, while the essential faith is available to anyone who believes, are not certain practices (like baptism and communion) available only to the initiates?

Remember what I said that many people willfully persist in ignorance. This is cognitive bias. At some point along the way, a person sets up a persistent unconscious thought process as a protection against a threat to their identity. At 17, I told myself that I could never be a creative writer, and that was self-trauma to my identity. Sometimes people act out of their trauma. Their safety is threatened so they adopt a cognitive bias against practices that may be beneficial to them but threaten their identity. Consequently, they set up a little lie about how yoga and meditation are not Christ-like and will cause weaker brothers to stumble. This is a lie based on cognitive bias and willful ignorance.

Because I grew up in conservative sects of Christianity, I never considered yoga and meditation until my forties. I heard the admonitions against these occultic practices and dismissed them out of hand. Nevertheless, I was so desperate to not go back to the place where I was in 2012, I told God that I was going to try yoga and meditation in an attempt to draw closer to him. I also said this to him: AS ABOVE, SO BELOW.

    I prayed to God that *maybe* the blue-haired ladies at church were wrong when they told me that meditation and yoga would lead to drawing pentagrams on the floor and summoning demons. I told God that if demon-summoning or anything like it ever happened in any instruction I received in yoga or meditation, I would flee. After five years of yoga and three of meditation, these things have never happened. Yoga and meditation have only drawn me closer to my source. My Christian God has blessed me by meeting me in yoga and meditation. While these practices will not help me get to heaven, these practices are specific and focused ways, like prayer, for me to let Jesus shine through me because he lives inside my heart.

Chapter 24

Modern American Christianity—Part 2

Just as is the case with yoga and meditation, the Christian church needs to reckon with cannabis and natural psychedelics. The church now looks with great skepticism on these plant-based medicines because of their past association with "pagan" religious practices. In the past, it also has been easy for the church to dismiss cannabis and psychedelics because they were illegal to possess.

Paul advocates civil obedience in the Book of Romans from the New Testament. Without direct experience of how therapeutic something like psilocybin-containing mushrooms can be, or without a willingness to consider science, it is easy to dismiss psychedelics, and perceive them only in the way the government describes them, as more dangerous than heroin, methamphetamine, cocaine, or even alcohol. This attitude almost seems to be recommended by Paul because of his arguments about obedience to the law.

I mentioned The Immortality Key by Brian C. Muraresku. In this book, Brian presents strong evidence that the ancient pagan psychedelic rituals from Greece and elsewhere were practiced alongside Christianity in the first centuries of its existence as a religion. Brian suggests that it is time for the church to reclaim these gifts of creation to help heal trauma and inspire belief. The church could reclaim these tools to help heal trauma regardless of belief, but I think that men and women may believe differently after having the same powerful experiences with psychedelics that I had. My experiences are not unique.

My dad and other theologians and pastors would tell you that true reformation and revival in the church begins with repentance, not with psilocybin mushrooms. There is a notion that God's people can repent of their sin and self-reliance and draw closer to God to get more in line with his plan. While I am not a pastor and do not want to be, I could be a lay person facilitator of all of the practices I describe here. I believe that if the church tried to feed and house the poor, teach meditation and yoga, heal trauma, and advise people on how to build heart-centered wealth, these practices could communicate Jesus' love unconditionally. I will leave the calls to repentance and revival to the pastors and evangelists. I think that Jesus' message was most powerful when he took actions as opposed to speaking words. He did both of course.

Christians' suspicion of psychedelics is not entirely unfounded. The Christian New Testament includes warnings against *pharmakeia*, the Greek word for "sorceries". In the Book of Revelations 18.23, men turn away from God because they are deceived by the *pharmakeia* of Babylon. In the Book of Galatians 5.19-20, Paul condemns sorcery using the Greek word *pharmakeia*. The specific language of the entire passage is instructive to understand the real intent of his words:

> The acts of the flesh are obvious: sexual immorality, impurity and debauchery; idolatry and witchcraft [*pharmakeia*]; hatred, discord, jealousy, fits of rage, selfish ambition, dissensions, factions and envy; drunkenness, orgies, and the like. I warn you, as I did before, that those who live like this will not inherit the kingdom of God.

It is obvious that *pharmakeia* is the root word for "pharmaceutical", and apart from sorcery, most lexicons give the first definitions of the word as "the use or administration of drugs" or "poisoning". Importantly, apart from these definitions, an alternative meaning is "idolatry". Idolatry has to do with worshiping other gods, and the human mind can make a god of anything.

Idolatry is how *pharmakeia* is translated in this passage (along with witchcraft).

Some Christians interpret these passages as condemning any use of pharmaceuticals, that any use of prescription medicine violates God's laws.

These considerations are legitimate because to properly practice Christianity, you are instructed to "pick sides". The direction from the Torah in Deuteronomy 6.4, "Hear, O Israel: The LORD is our God, the LORD is one!" precludes the worship of any other gods, including relying on our own efforts or understanding. This was Israel's commandment, but it continues to have relevance for Christians because Jesus said that it was the most important commandment in the Gospel of Mark 12.29. I personally do not want to seek out any other gods in my practice of Christianity. It only would bring me confusion. I would not recommend my Christian brothers or sisters to seek out other gods either. I believe Jesus is sufficient.

The distinction that I would make to understand the warnings about *pharmakeia* is the same one that Christians use to justify taking prescription medicines. How can we be engaging in paganism (turning to other gods) if we perceive a medicine as an agent for healing that God created?

If we take medicine with the intent of communicating with demons or spirits, that would be the wrong use of medicine. It would be unusual to perceive that you have the ability to commune with spirits after taking antibiotics, but many people report encountering entities, aliens, and machine elves after ingesting DMT or psilocybin. These "demons" could be projections of my own consciousness, but they certainly could be real demons I suppose. Do I encounter demons when I dream? From this perspective, I appreciate the warnings in the New Testament against *pharmakeia* because I can imagine how psychedelics could be used to attempt to engage with these entities. If the entities are demons and I smoke DMT with the purpose of interacting with the machine elves, that may indicate that I am consulting with foreign gods. This is certainly a topic for another book.

If my intent is on glorifying God and enjoying him forever, and to bring health to my life so that I can serve my community, I should be able to take antibiotics and be confident I am not engaging in demonology. I can also take psilocybin with the same intent. If I perceive it as a natural psychopharmaceutical that could alleviate persistent depression and anxiety, as long my intention in taking the medicine is that I would be directed toward God and not to communicate with demons (or angels or spirits), could it be wrong? This is almost too obvious to have to describe, but it is necessary for Christians to consider in the context of natural psychedelics. It is important because the church could take a role in healing trauma through implementing practices like the Marsh Chapel Experiment, an experiment in 1962 where psilocybin was administered to Harvard divinity students.

There is a passage from my source text with which some Protestants may not be familiar. The sect of Christianity that I most closely identify with is Protestantism. Many Christians (including Protestants) do not really know the Bible, or only have a vague notion of everything that it says. I can't claim to have total knowledge of the contents of the Bible, but I have read it cover to cover a few times and specific parts of it many times.

The Bible is a long book. In fact, one of the other major Christian sects that you may have heard of, Catholicism, has a different Bible from Protestantism because it includes additional books making it even longer. One of these additional books of the Bible that is "extra-canonical" to Protestants is the Book of Sirach, also known as the Wisdom of Sirach, also known as the Book of Ecclesiasticus (not to be confused with Ecclesiastes!).

For purposes of this chapter, I would commend the Book of Sirach to my fellow Christians whose consciences have ever been pricked by taking prescription medicines, thinking they were violating Paul's prohibition against *pharmakeia*. Sirach, Chapter 38, verses 1 through 8 are quoted in their entirety below (from the New Revised Standard Version):

> Honor physicians for their services, for the Lord created them; for their gift of healing comes from the Most High, and they are rewarded by the king. The skill of physicians makes them distinguished, and in the presence of the great they are admired. *The Lord created medicines out of the earth, and the sensible will not despise them* [emphasis added]. Was not water made sweet with a tree in order that its power might be known? And he gave skill to human beings that he might be glorified in his marvelous works. By them the physician heals and takes away pain; the pharmacist makes a mixture from them. God's works will never be finished; and from him health spreads over all the earth.

I picked psilocybin-containing mushrooms growing wild in a cow pasture in the most geographically-remote place in the world, Hawaii. These psychedelic mushrooms grow EVERYWHERE! I cannot help but believe that God created these mushrooms as natural psychopharmaceuticals. Do you think that the ancients did not know about them? Undoubtedly, early Christians knew about the ancient Greek pagan rituals, the Mysteries of Dionysus, and the Temple of Eleusis. It would be supremely arrogant of us as moderns to think that it is only now in the 20th and 21st centuries that we are beginning to interact with psychedelics. That is why Brian Muraresku's book is so important. Now, in the 21st century science is proving that psilocybin is far safer and more effective than manufactured prescription drugs. What is most remarkable is that psilocybin grows from the ground.

When the man-made drugs proved ineffective for me, and when my sacred text tells me that medicine grows from the ground, do you think that I am going to obey a law that was enacted specifically to perpetuate racism in the United States and deprive myself of a healing agent? My legal justification for possessing cannabis, DMT, and psilocybin is based on medical necessity and religious liberty.

As is the case sometimes with the Bible, it seems to be self-contradictory, and in this instance, Paul's warnings and the warnings from the Book of Revelations against *pharmakeia* seem to contradict Sirach's approval of physicians and medicine. The only thing for the faithful to do is to attempt to harmonize the apparently contradictory passages. I want to try to be brief in this summary and not go into detailed descriptions of hermeneutic methods that my dad would be far more skilled at describing than me. The passage from Sirach and its commonsensical wisdom seem to give me permission to take medicines that grow "out of the earth". I will be "sensible" if I do "not despise them."

As I have mentioned before, the plant medicines that I ingested and that have given me the greatest healing (cannabis, DMT, and psilocybin) have all drawn me closer to my Christian God. I believe that my faith in Jesus has only deepened through my ingestion of psychedelics. I have experienced an expansion in my capacity for love and for empathy, and that makes me really happy. I no longer want to kill myself. Psychedelics gave me a real sense of how it feels to be loved by God.

What the Marsh Chapel Experiment (and other experiments just like it) showed is that mystical experiences induced by psilocybin are just as legitimate to the people who experienced them as non-induced mystical experiences. How can that be a bad thing? There is a notion of "relying on the arm of flesh" in Paul (as described above in the discussion of Galatians), but in the context of psilocybin, that is a spiritualized way to recommend that I turn away from common sense. This is a way of justifying someone's cognitive bias based on willful ignorance, to forbid something that may be tremendously useful, and in fact, the one thing that really can heal something like persistent depression, PTSD, or anxiety.

My use of psilocybin drew me away from "[t]he acts of the flesh". Since ingesting psychedelics, I have gained new perspectives on pornography and sexual abstinence. I have largely quit drinking alcohol. I have reengaged in my Christian faith. I spend hours at a time, sometimes daily, with the scriptures in my art (the T. H. Chalm Bible Poetry I described earlier). My feelings of anger and discord with my ex-wife have reduced. I am less jealous, less envious, I have fewer instances where my temper gets the better of me. My ambition has been redirected, and I seek out unity rather than division. I believe all these things have occurred by the power of God (Jesus) working through me, and one of the main ways that they have occurred is because I obeyed Sirach's encouragement to be sensible. Sirach 38.4 says that "sensible" people will not despise them," with the "them" referring to the "medicines out of the earth" that "[t]he Lord created."

Because I did not invoke demons, angels, or spirits, I took psilocybin just like most people take Prozac, and with the same intention that I have when I take antibiotics. Most Christians would not bat an eye Prozac or antibiotics, and why? Because they took the commonsense approach of trusting their doctors.

My doctor could not prescribe psilocybin, though, because it is illegal to possess. It is also a plant-like organism (a mushroom) that grows from the ground. The legal issue has been remedied in some places. Several municipalities (Denver, Ann Arbor, Santa Cruz, to name a few) have decriminalized psilocybin-containing mushrooms. If there is no law against the mushrooms, couldn't they be treated similarly to medical cannabis?

Everyone knows about how the status of cannabis

has shifted in the United States. I first obtained a recommendation for medical cannabis from a doctor in California in 2010. I provided my medical records showing that I had tried at least three other prescription psychopharmaceuticals for depression and anxiety and told the doctor that none of them helped as much as cannabis. He gave me a "recommendation" (not a prescription) to take cannabis for my symptoms. While it was not a prescription, the imprimatur of a doctor was relevant when I was measuring my conduct against God's word.

    The point here is, couldn't the same thing be done with psilocybin-containing mushrooms? The psychedelic effects of psilocybin are substantially more pronounced than the effects of cannabis. I would recommend a greater degree of care when consuming psilocybin as compared with cannabis. Note that through microdosing, it is *easy* to experience psilocybin's healing potential in a gentle and completely safe way. The main safety issue with psilocybin is that if you take a large enough dose, you will be severely disoriented for a few hours, you would be unable to drive, and you may have some impulses to do nonsensical things that a trip sitter can help redirect. If you read about experiences with psilocybin, you will learn that the only real supervision that is required is from a friend, not a doctor. A trip sitter is adequate to help facilitate a safe experience with psilocybin. This is how medically safe psilocybin is.

The church could take an active role in helping facilitate healing rituals with psilocybin just like the Marsh Chapel Experiment, also known as the "Good Friday Experiment". If you have not read about this, it provides an example of how the church could lead psychedelic healing rituals.

Many people have heard of Timothy Leary and Ram Dass (Richard Alpert), both of whom were professors at Harvard University in the 1960s. Their popularity (or notoriety) arose from their association and advocacy of the use of natural psychedelics and LSD as healing agents for mental health issues. One experiment that they conducted involved giving psilocybin to prisoners (the Concord Prison Experiment) and measuring recidivism rates. They conducted extensive research in the use of psychedelics as healing agents until 1970's United States federal Controlled Substances Act classified psychedelic medicines (including cannabis) as more dangerous than heroin, methamphetamine, and cocaine. Because of their supposed danger, possession of psychedelic plants was severely criminalized at the U.S. federal level, and the states followed suit. Alcohol, determined to be the most dangerous drug by the Lancet study, has been completely legal in the United States since the end of Prohibition in the 1930s.

In association with Leary's and Alpert's research, Walter N. Pahnke, a graduate student in theology at Harvard Divinity School, designed an experiment where psilocybin would be given to a group of divinity students to determine whether the medicine could initiate a mystical experience in religiously inclined persons. The experiment was conducted in 1962 on Good Friday at Boston University's Marsh Chapel with ten participants receiving psilocybin and ten receiving a placebo. Almost all the participants in the study who took psilocybin reported having profound religious experiences. One of the participants, Huston Smith (who went on to author multiple textbooks on comparative religion) described the experience as "the most powerful cosmic homecoming I have ever experienced."

I described the Ayahuasca ceremonies in which I participated. All a church would need to do is provide a safe place, and it could facilitate similar trauma healing retreats with psilocybin. The dosage on my cannabis recommendation was "as needed". With volunteer trip sitters, the church could help people heal trauma without requiring anything in return. How do you think people would respond to that kind of unconditional love? If the church could take an active role in binding up the wounds of mental illness in this way, don't you think that it would have a greater place of relevance in our culture? Wouldn't that be a way to redeem the evils that have been done in the name of Jesus? What if the Catholic church could hold PTSD healing rituals for people who have been traumatized by pedophile priests? This could be accomplished with a natural substance (a mushroom) that is medically as dangerous as coffee, or something that you might put in a salad or spaghetti.

    The main danger from psychedelics is that they remain illegal to possess in many jurisdictions. If their possession were decriminalized, with minimal supervision, psilocybin ceremonies could be safely conducted at churches by lay (non-clergy) volunteers. It is simply a matter of reforming the laws first, and our will, understanding, and appreciation of God's word next. The church can facilitate healing mental illness just like Jesus did with the miracle of the demon-possessed man (the "exorcism of the Gerasene demoniac" described in the Gospels of Mark and Luke) who undoubtedly was suffering from (at least) severe complex PTSD.

Chapter 25
Real Estate and Leveraged Returns

Real estate is fundamental to Real Advisers.

As a heart-centered advisory practice, we are irrelevant unless we have useful knowledge that enables everyone at every economic level and level of life satisfaction: the low income earners; the high income earners; the poor; the wealthy; the happy; the sad; everyone. I wanted to reach everyone in my work and that is what The Offer has allowed me to achieve as a middle-aged corporate and securities attorney. I have transformed myself into a meditation and psychedelic evangelist and heart-centered wealth advisor!

Real estate is fundamental to Real Advisers because every night, you and I must meet a fundamental need that all of humanity shares. Even before we die from thirst or starvation, we likely will sleep, and when we sleep, where will we lay our head? You may be sleeping outside now, as many of the homeless in Austin and throughout the United States will tonight. You may be in a mansion in Westlake, or as blessed as the wealthiest man in Austin (me) who leases a home that his mom owns as an investment property, a four-bedroom single family home behind the best bowling alley south of Lady Bird Lake. No matter who you are, tonight you will lay your head down to rest somewhere.

Wherever that place is, Real Advisers will ask you whether you are using real estate as a tool to advance your goal of wealth creation? If you are starting from scratch, you simultaneously want to meet your need for a place to sleep by creating an investment vehicle for yourself. This investment vehicle could earn you a 27% or greater investment return over the next year. In this chapter, I will give you a specific example about how we did this with the house my mom bought as an investment property.

Before I describe that, it will be useful to describe leveraged returns outside of the context of real estate. You may be most familiar with the concept of leveraged returns when you think about buying stock on margin.

Let's say I just read the news (on Reddit of course) that Apple announced the iPhone *13* as a surprise, because they decided to skip over the number 12. I read about this news early in the morning and decide that on that day, I am going to capitalize on what I am certain will be an inevitable price appreciation (increase) with Apple's stock. Everyone will be so excited about this random surprise event in the news (the iPhone 13) and how they perceive it makes Apple more valuable, they will rush to buy Apple stock. The increase in demand drives the per share price up. I want to buy at a price in the morning that will be much lower than what I anticipate the price will be later in the day because of all the trading activity based on this news.

This strategy is known as event-driven trading. An event, the surprise announcement of the iPhone 13, occurred and you believe that this event will have a specific effect on price movement of a stock that day. If you accurately can predict price movements, you can capitalize on that knowledge to make profits through trading public company stocks.

I have tried to implement this strategy on my own, and it is very difficult. After about six months, I decided that I was simply not knowledgeable enough about the market to be successful in this strategy. I perceived that there were so many unknown (to me) forces and unpredictable effects in the markets that I would be better off focusing on the practice of law and investing in real estate. This is not to say that event-driven trading is not a valid trading strategy. In fact, it can be an effective trading strategy if it is employed by people with greater experience and knowledge of the markets than me. Further, it is possible that Real Advisers may sponsor an event-driven fund in the future. For the moment though we are focusing on real estate.

Let's say that I can buy a share of Apple for $100 today (I checked and today's opening price in early October 2020 is $114.97, so $100 would be a bargain!). Let's imagine that I just read the news about the new iPhone 13 and immediately knew that there would be upwards price movement in the share price TODAY. I would invest quickly. I logged into my online brokerage account and used the $100 I had saved during the last month since I quit drinking to buy one share of Apple at $100.

Sure enough, as I predicted, by the end of the day, the market was so excited about the iPhone 13, the price of the one share I bought had increased in value to $110. This is a 10% price appreciation in a day, and if that continued for a year, it would result in an annual return in excess of 400%! You quickly could invest and retire earning that rate of return on a consistent basis. I decide to bank my returns at the end of the day and sell the share, making $10 in the process. It represents a 10% one day return, but it is only $10.

Please note that for much of this discussion, we are ignoring transaction costs and taxes on capital gains for the sake of describing what leveraged returns are. These taxes and transaction costs are both very real and relevant and effectively would reduce the amount of the net gains described here. I try to give you good examples and note where we can use estimated transaction costs to give better representations of the actual expected returns.

Getting back to my example with Apple, what if I thought to take my $100 and borrow $900 from my online broker, and invest a total of $1,000 in 10 shares of Apple? Then at the end of the day, I have achieved profits of $100 ($10, the price appreciation on one share, multiplied by ten (10) for each of the shares I bought with the $1,000). The broker will charge you a day's interest on this margin loan, but for purposes of this exercise, let's say that that one day's interest and fees were $0. They won't be zero, but it will be easier for the sake of our discussion of leveraged returns to ignore them for the time being.

Because I invested my $100, and combined it with $900 that I borrowed, running the same event-driven strategy regarding Apple resulted in $100 of profits rather than $10. I doubled my money in a day. Those are

TERRIFIC returns. I was able to double my money because I achieved the investment returns on 10 shares when I only had enough to buy one. The broker is happy because I repaid the $900 loan to them and I am happy because I had a 2X day!

But what if I were wrong about this expected increase in the price of Apple, and the market did not respond as I thought? What if everyone thought it was a terrible idea that Apple *ever* would have an iPhone 13 because everyone knows that triskaidekaphobia (fear of the number 13) is a thing? Apple should have done their research before proceeding with this supposedly great idea. Instead of the $10 per share increase, the stock price declines 10% that day to $90. If I had just invested my $100, I would have had a loss of $10 on the day (if I sold the share). If I held the share of Apple, I would own something worth $90 that I had purchased at the beginning of the day for $100. Knowing the general price movements of Apple, I would probably decide to hold that share and wait for the price to go back up, but maybe not.

What if I had bought the 10 shares on margin using the borrowed $900. I would now have 10 shares worth $900, and I have a $900 margin loan due to the broker immediately. I could give the 10 shares back to the broker (now worth $900) and be done with the entire thing. I totally forgot that people think that the number 13 is unlucky! In this case, you started the day with $100 and ended the day with $0. You lost all your money that you had saved from not drinking. Bummer! Please don't start drinking again.

Your losses were exacerbated because you borrowed money to buy the stock. Buying stock on margin is a horrible idea unless you really know what you are doing.

Part of the problem with buying stock on margin is the potential high volatility with respect to stock share prices (they can go up and down a lot in a single day). The interest charges on the margin loans are high and they are short term, so I owe that $900 NOW even though I still want to hold on to my hapless 10 shares.

What if there were an asset where the margin loan could be long-term (maybe 30 years) and its interest rate was much lower? Part of the reason that the interest rate is set high on stock margin loans is risk of default related to intrinsic market risk. What if margin loans on this other class had the more favorable terms because this other asset class had much less volatility in price and also was a class of assets that are made up of things that you could touch and feel (and maybe even meet some of your fundamental needs with) rather than something abstract like a share of stock? Of course, you know I am referring to real estate.

When my mom bought the house I am renting from her, she used margin (leverage). The house cost $300,000 (in Austin this was a bargain!) and she paid $60,000 as a down payment. She obtained a mortgage loan with a fixed rate of around 4% and a 30-year term. This is an incredibly low interest rate and a great term. This was a solid buy and my mom believes she made a good investment decision.

I found some free data showing that Austin single family homes appreciated 67% in the last 10 years. Let's just say that for the sake of simplicity, the average annual price appreciation that you can expect from a home in Austin is 7%. (This is an over-simplification, but the whole point of this is to demonstrate the value of using margin on the purchase of a safe asset like a single-family home in Austin's admittedly "hot" real estate market.)

Let's take my mom's house as an example. Let's say that she bought the house using all cash. She bought a house at the beginning of the year for $300,000 and now because of the price appreciation she has a house worth $321,000 ($300,000*7%=$21,000). She can sell and pocket the difference. If she does it through a title company and pays agents on both sides of the sale, after taxes, it's not a bad trade, but her net gain is much less than 7% because of the transaction costs. This is an important point, and you should never forget transaction costs with real estate (just like with stock trading).

This is not the way my mom bought her house though. Remember? She used a $240,000 margin loan (a mortgage) to buy the house. She invested $60,000, but still obtained the appreciation on $300,000. At the end of the year, if she sold, she would get her $60,000 back, plus the $21,000 appreciation (net of transaction costs mentioned above). Let's say that after transaction costs, she made $8,000 in profit. A $60,000 investment making a $8,000 return in a year represents an annual return of around 13%! I do not suffer from triskaidekaphobia and nearly everyone I know would be ecstatic with a 13% return. That is a really good investment return by any measure.

The ability to achieve safe leveraged returns on real estate investments is a fundamental principle that

Real Advisers wants to help our clients implement to achieve outsized returns even greater than 13%. The example I gave above was a good deal, but it wasn't *really* great. What's a really great deal?

The example I gave above assumed an 80% debt-to-value ratio (meaning that my mom paid 20% cash as a down payment). What if she were able to do the same transaction using 10% down and a 90% loan. In that case she would have made a $30,000 investment but still obtained the same $8,000 return. That represents a 27% return. That is OUTSTANDING!! These are the returns that we are going to be targeting for our investors at Real Advisers.

Worth mentioning is that you can also calculate the return if you put no money down, a 0% down payment. Many people do not think that this is possible, and while it is difficult, it has been done before. The returns on an investment that requires no cash can be calculated, and when you calculate them, they are infinite. Remember what I said about how your rate is higher than Bill Gates'? Even if you just make the infinite return on the one deal, that is your potential.

We all know about what happened in the world in 2020 with COVID-19, but nevertheless, the Austin residential real estate market has stayed strong. With everyone realizing the freedom that working from home provides, anyone who ever said that they would move to Austin if only they did not have to stay located in their current city for their job are seeing that they can continue on in their current position and also live in Austin. Oracle, Tesla, Elon Musk, and Joe Rogan all just moved here. The "hotness" of Austin (and how "cool" it is to live here) has been a thing for a "minute" (as the kids say).

Let's say that we live in a market where the price appreciation is lower, or let's assume that something unexpected happens in Austin or the overall economy, and this causes prices in residential real estate to decline in one year by 7%. That has happened in certain residential real estate markets in the past, but it is rare and the values always come back.

If that one-year decline occurs, I am disappointed, but what have I been doing with my investment that entire time? I have been sleeping in it. I sleep great here. There is a barking chihuahua in the neighbor's back yard, but they scrupulously observe Austin's 10 p.m. to 7 a.m. noise ordinance. I have been sleeping less recently since the idea for The Offer came my way. Even though I did not achieve the profits that I thought I possibly could, I still own (or have a right to live in) the house. Even though the value declined, I can comfort myself that if I live here for a little while, the value inevitably will appreciate again to exceed my purchase price. The most important thing to remember is that I have a roof over my head which is something that a share of Apple cannot give me.

The prior paragraph is about risk mitigation. It is impossible to eliminate risk in your investment decisions. Asset prices always depend on factors that are completely outside of your control. Nevertheless, your risk mitigation strategy can ensure that you will have a place to sleep tonight.

After investing in single family homes on your own, you can take the next step. Let's combine 100+ one-bedroom to three-bedroom residential units into a single asset and through efficiencies of scale obtain even higher returns. Real Advisers will help you invest in privately syndicated multi-family and other commercial real estate assets to achieve outsized returns. We can use margin to buy into this safe asset class that historically has achieved the best risk adjusted returns as measured by the Sharpe ratio. Overall, commercial real estate outperforms all other asset classes on a risk adjusted basis.

This is the literally grounding principle of Real Advisers, and I make the pun intentionally. We will help you do this on your own to achieve your own outsized investment returns. Further, as a part time representative, you can learn how to help your friends do this in the context of a heart-centered investment advisory practice that focuses on TRUE wealth as we have defined it in this book.

To help you invest directly in real estate, we will recommend that you engage with Phill and Shenoah Grove with Austin's Real Estate Networking Club and Canis Major Incubator, LLC, a commercial real estate investment incubator. Phill and Shenoah help people by training them to invest in residential and commercial real estate safely to achieve the kinds of returns I describe above. There are varying strategies to employ depending on your wants and who you are, and how you can best serve your community, so I recommend you read this book first and then go talk to Phill and Shenoah.

Another business that we support in Austin is Adventum Funds. Adventum is an asset manager focusing on Austin commercial real estate. We plan on looking closely at deals that Adventum is making available and I foresee recommending their deals to our clients.

If you are tempted to go back and get your real estate license as a second career, that is not a bad idea. Alternatively, I would really recommend that you study for the Series 65 and come work with Real Advisers to help yourself and your community GROW WEALTHY.

One of the great things about working with Real Advisers is that you do not have to make any changes to your current career. If you want to be a real estate agent, plan on showing houses on the weekends and working very hard to build your practice in an entirely new business that you have never done before. You are not the only one thinking of real estate as a second career either. Tons of people flock to the real estate industry when they are thinking about alternative professions. This is not a bad idea, particularly if you are natural extrovert and think that it would be fun to work with people who are regularly making what probably will be the most significant financial decision of their lives, not based on logic and reason, but based on strong feelings and emotions. We are doing that with Real Advisers too, but first we are giving them a copy of this book to read to help them manage their emotions and make sure that they are making decisions that are in their financial best interests.

Being a residential real estate agent sounds exhausting to me since I am an introvert by nature and the thought of entering an entirely new business is not appealing. This is why I created Real Advisers instead.

If you are a nurse, you could be a Real Advisers financial advisor to other healthcare professionals at your workplace. The Offer is a unique gamifiable lead generation and team building tool that allows you to engage with people in an inoffensive way. The Offer allows you to share your own core personal values with people around you as an invitation to true friendship. You will be asking them to share their responses to The Task in a way that will help you grow in intimacy, just like I grew in intimacy with my dad when I really appreciated for the first time how important gardening was to him. Your invitation to them will include sharing our app with them. If they consider anything written in The Offer, or maybe even just read the poem, they may be encouraged to think about their financial goals in a more heart-centered way. Not only will they be serving their own interests, but in the process, they will be thinking about service and how they can engage better with their community. Community means the interests of others, but in community, other people inevitably start helping to look after YOUR OWN interests. Community creates a self-serving positive feedback loop if you position yourself as a giver.

    I have described in this book that thinking these thoughts is necessary before achieving the wealth that my source text calls "blessed", which means to be rich in money and community, to both possess wealth and enjoy it. I am truly a blessed man and I want to help others become as blessed through the work that I am doing on The Offer.

Chapter 26

Federal Income Tax Planning

One of the things that Real Advisers will encourage you to do immediately is form your own business. We and our affiliated service partners can advise you about how to manage and run it as well. We will not always encourage you to quit your "day job" immediately, but understanding how you can own and operate your own business in different contexts can be a great aid in helping you plan for United States federal income tax minimization. It also can be a way for you to quit your job if that is what you want. As mentioned before, starting your own business can be a great way for you to create a community.

While I am not certain about the tax regimes in other parts of the world, I assume that similar planning strategies to the ones I describe here exist in other counties. The reason for this assumption is that the income tax laws in every country are written by the rich (i.e., the people with large bank accounts whether they are wealthy or not) to favor their interests.

I mentioned before that so long as you are working for earned income, whether it is for your business or somebody else, it is impossible for you to keep 100% of your money and comply completely with the provisions of the Internal Revenue Code. This is the case because under the United States federal income tax law you at least must pay yourself a reasonable salary (even if you own your own business) and that salary always will be subject to withholding of employment taxes (Social Security, employment, and Medicare). What I am going to describe in this chapter are some things that I've done for myself and my own business, Wiederaenders Law Firm, PLLC, to help reduce taxes. There are certain limitations on the ownership of Subchapter "S" corporations (no non-U.S. persons, no entity ownership) that may mean that Real Advisers will be taxed as a partnership for now, but we may later convert to a corporation if we were going to receive equity financing or if we were going to conduct an IPO. At any rate, what I am describing in this chapter with respect to the personal services Subchapter "S" corporation planning applies generally to people like me, individuals in the United States running personal services firms.

The following could apply to any personal or professional services firm, whether it is owned and operated by a plumber, electrician, engineer, masseuse, or whatever. This is applicable to anybody that owns their own business and who performs services in connection with that business. For my business I formed a limited liability company (an "LLC") which is the most commonly used type of business entity in the United States.

    LLCs have four options with respect to how they can be taxed. Without making any election with the IRS, a 100% owned LLC will be deemed a "disregarded entity" and all tax items will flow through to the 100% owner (the sole member). The tax items will be reported on an individual sole member's Form 1040 Schedule C. Second, if owned by two or more unrelated persons, an LLC will be taxed as a partnership, and in a similar fashion, the tax items will be reported separately to the owners pro rata in accordance with their ownership percentages. The third option is that the LLC may elect to be taxed as a corporation under Subchapter "C" of the Internal Revenue Code. Subchapter "C" corporations are how most large publicly traded companies are organized, and there are specific reasons for this that go beyond the scope of this book. The fourth option is that after the LLC has made the election to be taxed as a corporation under Subchapter "C", it can make the further election to be taxed as a corporation under Subchapter "S" of the Code. Subchapter "S" allows corporations to be taxed like partnerships. For purposes of our discussion, the second and fourth options are so similar that they will result in substantially the same tax results.

To achieve the results I am describing here as a single-member LLC you must pick the fourth option, and elect to be taxed as a Subchapter "C" corporation first, and then a Subchapter "S" corporation. Please note that nothing in this is tax or legal advice. I am describing things in very general terms but to implement these strategies, I highly recommend that you discuss them with a tax attorney or accountant. These professionals frequently will give you free consultations. Try to find someone that you "click" with personally and who immediately encourages you rather than attempts to dissuade you from taking the steps I am describing here.

I want to describe how my law firm works from a tax perspective. Gross revenues are what I receive from client billing collections. My law firm pays me a W-2 salary and on a quarterly basis withholds employment taxes, paying them to the IRS via their Electronic Federal Tax Payment System (EFTPS). My firm also pays for all its expenses, and I will tell you more about those below. These include things like costs of my internet, cell phone, and contractors I hire to work for me. Whatever is left over after paying my salary and the expenses is paid to me as profits.

First, note that the law firm expenses are deductible against gross income and reduce the amount of income that is subject to tax. Reducing the amount of income that is subject to tax is how you achieve the goal of reducing taxes. This is a very important concept in tax law and if you are not familiar with how the tax law works, there are many good resources that can explain it better. In fact, the IRS guides themselves can be very instructive, and people like tax lawyers actually read things like Revenue and Private Letter Rulings that the IRS issues as guidance about specific tax questions. The IRS should not always be viewed as the enemy. They are simply attempting to administer the tax code, and sometimes they do it correctly. Sometimes they make mistakes. Contrary to what you may believe, or what you may have experienced, IRS employees are human beings just like you and me.

Your salary will be subject to employment tax which creates a withholding obligation for your firm. Social security, Medicare, and employment taxes on your wages/salary at least must be withheld quarterly and paid to the IRS.

To repeat what I mentioned above, my firm's profits are calculated by taking gross revenue (billings) and deducting expenses (including my salary and the other expenses I described). The most important thing to note in this discussion of personal services Subchapter "S" corporations is that the profits are only taxed at the ordinary income tax rate. Additional employment taxes are not tacked on like they are with your salary. Your salary is always taxed at the ordinary income tax rate and you also pay the employment taxes (which you don't pay on profits).

You may think, "why don't I just pay myself a low, low salary and I'll take out the rest as profits not subject to employment tax?" This is a very good idea, but the IRS thought of this too. Their answer is that you must pay yourself a "reasonable" salary. Ideally you would survey all the service providers in your area, both professionally and geographically, and determine what an average salary would be for you including factors such as the type of work you perform and your level of experience. This is a difficult technical analysis and is unfair for the IRS to require, since to accurately determine what a reasonable salary should be for me, I would have to commission a detailed economic study that probably would cost at least $5,000. That is an unreasonable and unnecessary expense for a small business, yet that may be the only way for you to truly document that you paid yourself a reasonable salary. If you ever fight the IRS in District Court or Tax Court, you may have to commission a study like that to win.

Everybody should determine a reasonable salary on their own. One guideline that I heard recently (from a fellow attorney) is to take gross revenues and divide that by three. One third will be paid as salary, one third is paid as expenses, and the remainder is profits. If the firm is paying quarterly taxes on the salary, at the end of the year, it calculates expenses and whatever is left over will be profits taxed at the ordinary income tax rate (but not subject to employment taxes). I am not an accountant and this is not legal advice, but this seems like a fairly practical way of running a business generally. It is not dissimilar to the approach that I took in my own business.

Being unable to provide a table of reasonable salaries here for each profession (which would be voluminous), I would encourage you to discuss with your accountants what they think about this. Please note that all things being equal, accountants and attorneys will give you advice that will tend to be more conservative. The salary amount they suggest is one that they believe the IRS certainly would not deem unreasonably low. I'm not saying not to rely on their advice but know that you can set your own salary. If your accountant truly believes you are violating the law, they will refuse to perform services or file your return. They will let you know, and at that point, either listen to their advice or find a new accountant. Personally, I am more aggressive than my accountant. Nevertheless, she just filed my Form 1120S corporate return and Form 1040 individual return for 2019 and agreed to keep working with me in the future. I must be doing something right.

Again, all of this is personal recollection, I am not an accountant, and this not legal advice though I am an attorney. I really recommend that you get your own accountant and attorney so that you can talk through these matters with them. They likely will give you a free consultation initially and you should be able to assess whether the person you are talking to can help you with these matters quickly. You can even give them a copy of this book for reference.

Another tax advantage to a personal services Subchapter "S" corporation is the ability to deduct certain expenses that you cannot when you are a disregarded entity. Discuss this with an accountant also, but I guarantee this is a thing. There are definite tax benefits to having your own personal services firm taxed as a Subchapter "S" corporation rather than a disregarded entity and reporting revenue and expenses from your business on your 1040.

What I describe to you above takes some planning and probably requires you to hire an accountant (but maybe not). It is relatively simple to do if you already own your own business. If you do not, there are still ways of creating businesses that may generate great tax planning opportunities for you.

Do you remember when I told you about the Merciful Gardener Foundation Inc. (MGF) that I created with some friends? Using nonprofit and tax-exempt corporations is a way for you to deploy your resources to minimize tax liability and build up community.

MGF is a Texas nonprofit corporation. We applied to the IRS to qualify the corporation as a tax-exempt organization as described under Section 501(c)(3) of the Internal Revenue Code. This designation pertains to charitable organizations and is the same designation churches hold. Any donations that people now make to MGF are deductible against their income just like donations to churches. This is an important point to make. Most people face a choice of either paying income tax (not employment tax) to the IRS, or an equal amount to a charitable organization. Remember what I said about how you cannot keep all your money?

    The benefit to you of creating a charitable organization is that you can have a degree of control over its operations and philosophy. In Texas you must have three unrelated persons to serve on a board of directors of a nonprofit corporation. The nonprofit corporation is the most commonly used entity type for organizations seeking Section 501(c)(3) tax-exempt status. The board of directors really is independent so theoretically, two of the three could join up and fire you and take over the corporation. I would encourage people only doing this with friends that they really trust and respect and have great confidence that they will be able to work together on a team. I mentioned before about how you can create your own communities, and this is one of the best ways.

    Most people have some charitable purpose that

they wish they could support more, but year after year, continue to pay taxes to the IRS. With some planning, they probably could avoid paying those taxes by redirecting the same amount to charity. The biggest hurdle is having the necessary knowledge and counsel about how to do all this legally. You must incorporate and learn some corporate governance rules. There is a brief application you must file with the IRS, but I guarantee this effort will be well worth your time. You can simultaneously create tax planning opportunities and community. Consider forming a tax-exempt corporation. Real Advisers' affiliated law firm partners can assist you with these matters.

Remember when I wrote that I wanted advice about whether I should get my MFA? As I was writing this chapter, an idea occurred to me. Something I could do immediately (because I already did it with the Merciful Gardener Foundation) is create another Texas nonprofit, let's call it the "T. H. Chalm Poetry Education Foundation Inc." Its charitable purpose could be to further education by creating scholarship opportunities for underprivileged kids who want to study poetry or creative writing in college. Every dollar of mine contributed to this organization (subject to certain AGI limitations) would be deductible against my income. With those dollars combined with dollars that others contribute, we could create a scholarship fund to send kids to college to study creative writing. Wouldn't that be great? I know that 17-year-old Roland would have been interested in something like that.

An organization like this could help me build community with my family. I regularly inform my kids about my business. My kids know a lot about how I am attorney, and I also have told them about my creative writing. I always give them copies of my poetry books. They have encouraged me a lot with the Bible poetry and the gift of my poetry to them emphasizes how seriously I take my religion without preaching at them. As an aside, if you do not take your belief system seriously, maybe ask yourself why?

When I try to inform my children about what I do professionally, we have a signal for when they get bored. When I'm telling them about work and they raise their hand, I know then that I need to move on to a different topic or just stay quiet for a moment so they can have a chance to talk. I genuinely think that they are interested in the work I do as an attorney, and because of our discussions, they understand the law and corporate finance much better than any of their friends (even if they don't know it). This is the case because I try to give them full explanations about what it means to be a securities attorney. For example, I have described to them elements of a private offering of preferred stock and I force myself to put it in terms that they can understand.

When I talk with my children about my professional life, or inform them about my charitable activities, that is job training for them. Dialoguing with them is immensely valuable for me because they give me great feedback. Kids are smart! Describing complicated legal matters to them in terms that they can understand gives me a great teaching opportunity and it helps me better understand the topic. I identify new ideas, connections of thoughts, and ways of explaining things because I have talked about the law with my kids.

Just as is the case with any job training for an employee, the employer should pay the service provider for their time, so consequently my law firm pays my children for this job training that they're subjected to. This will be their only earned income for the year, and I can hire them as contractors. My 10-year-old son (who theoretically could have his own income tax return filing obligation) will receive a 1099 for whatever I pay him for the job training for all that time he listens to me talk about my work until he raises his hand. We open a bank account for him from which he can pay certain of his own expenses, such as food and housing. The law firm pays him salary that is deductible against law firm income and that amount goes into our joint account. In Texas this must be an "Underage Gift (To) Minors Account", or UGMA. Apart from his allowance, I take the balance of the account so he can reimburse me for his food and housing. This is completely legal. I have four kids, three of whom are under the age of 18. Until the amounts that you pay your children cause them to incur additional tax liability from other income sources, this can be a tax planning strategy even after they are 18.

  Another option is to create a business that revolves around a hobby. I formed a publishing company to self-publish my poems that few people read, but now my publishing company owns the rights to The Offer. I think my publishing company is going to get big over the next few years! It is going to have to pay me a reasonable salary and it may be hard to say that this salary should be low. This is just an example of a hobby that I turned into a business and now it has the potential to grow in a mighty way.

A final thought about nonprofits is to point out that some highly successful businesses like IKEA and Hershey's are owned by nonprofit corporations. Shortly after a time that a business is founded, the owner may wisely foresee that her business had the potential to continue to exist in perpetuity, or at least for a significant period after the founder's life. The founder wished to ensure the continued success of her corporation and its existence but wanted to plan for how her heirs would handle the corporation's stock that would pass to them on her death. She understood that they might not want to manage the corporation and could have other interests. She foresaw the possibility that her children might want to do different things with their lives than participate in the business in the same way as her. She foresaw wisely that they may inherit the stock and sell it all after her death, turning the corporation's control over to someone with different interests and intents.

The founder believes so strongly in the corporation and its purpose that she wanted to ensure a longer existence for it than if it had remained organized as a normal for-profit enterprise. To accomplish this, the founder contributed all of her stock in the corporation to a nonprofit corporation. By charter, she and members of her family would always have a right to fill seats on the Board of Directors of the nonprofit. In this way, they always would be guaranteed to have influence over how the business was run. While the founder and her family still can derive long-term benefits from the corporation (including prepaid annuities, housing, and employment arrangements), the founder cannot sell the corporation because all the shares of the corporation's stock are owned by the non-profit. The non-profit's board controls the composition of the for-profit subsidiary. The nonprofit even may pay taxes on a portion of its income. Still, the control of the independent board of the nonprofit is significant.

The use of a nonprofit corporation to own a for-profit's stock is an advanced intergenerational tax planning strategy that Real Advisers and its affiliated law firm partners can help you analyze further.

I also described how I am leasing a house that my mother owns. While she has many years left in her life, I also know that she shares the same fate that I do in that one day she and I both will die. That is reality. As it stands now, provided I stay in my mom's good graces, I will be her only heir and I will receive this house as an inheritance. It will be a tremendous blessing and it already is as I enjoy living here.

The IRS also acknowledges reality, and provides that upon her death, when I inherit the house, I will hold it with a tax basis equal to its fair market value at the time of her death.

We could have structured the purchase of this house in a different way. My mom could have given me $60,000 and I could have used that as a down payment to buy the house in my own name. (Ignore the gift tax issue as it is not relevant for the basis discussion.) At my mom's death there would be no tax effect with respect to my tax basis in the house. My tax basis would stay at $60,000 and when I sold it in the future anything that I received in excess of $60,000 would be taxed to me as capital gain.

Because my mom purchased the property, the tax effects will be different. Upon her death and the property passes to me through her will, I will inherit the property with a basis equal to its then-current fair market value. My mom bought this house for $300,000 in late 2018. Since then, Zillow informs me that its price has appreciated. Like I said, we got a good deal on this house and the Austin real estate market is a thing. The value has increased significantly over the past years even despite COVID-19. When I inherit my mom's house, my basis in the house will be equal to its fair market value on the date of her death, NOT $60,000.

The "step up" in basis at death is one of the most powerful tax planning strategies that can be employed. It is a dark joke among a tax attorneys and accountants that death is the best tax planning strategy. Of course, I am not counseling murder, but taking advantage of the tax results of death are a useful planning strategy that my mom and I are employing. If the tax code stays the same, I will do the same thing with my kids.

The point of this chapter is that you can take steps to structure your finances and living arrangements in a way that will work to your great economic advantage through tax planning. Many accountants and finance professionals simply either do not know about the tax planning strategies I am describing in this chapter (which are completely legal) or, because they do not place an emphasis on real estate or owning your own business, they do not provide you with advice or knowledge sufficient for you to do these things.

What I have described in this chapter requires you to work with attorneys and accountants. Understandably, many people may be apprehensive about incurring costs to hire attorneys and accountants. Nevertheless, with shifts in technology and increased work from home arrangements resulting from COVID-19, there will be more entrepreneurial attorneys and accountants in the future. This provides opportunities for buyers of their services.

One final tax planning strategy I wanted to mention has to do with my hand knotted rugs. One of the reasons I purchased these was because of the accelerated cost recovery provisions in the recent changes to the Code. It is very important for you to stay up to date with changes in the Code so that you can take full advantage of the strategies I am describing here. In addition to the rugs I bought some furniture that now graces my living room where my main office area is located. We also have places in the bedrooms for breakout meetings (remember I run a law firm from my house) and we have a break room in my kitchen. We can create spaces of comfortable privacy for multiple parties who may be present in person at my law firm to work on a transaction. I prepared my house for this event and bought couches for each of the bedrooms. I also bought a couch for my own bedroom so that I could have a place of privacy while my law firm employees might be working in the living room, the break room, or the other areas of my home office. The cost of these couches represented currently deductible expenses because they were purchased for the benefit of my home office.

Outside of this context, if you buy couches for your house, amounts paid for those couches are not deductible expenses. Because of the accelerated cost recovery rules, however, I was able to deduct the entire cost of these couches against the income that my business earned. It is not any different than me leasing an office from somebody and furnishing the office in the same way.

I would encourage you to begin to read the news about changes in the tax Code because I suspect over the next few years there will be significant changes that may be particularly relevant for all of us. No matter any future changes, there always will be ways to structure your finances with respect to the tax laws in a way that works to your economic advantage.

It is not illegal to arrange your financial affairs in

a way that works to your tax advantage. When thinking about these matters, never forget this dictum from Judge Learned Hand's opinion in the United States federal 2nd Circuit Court of Appeals case, *Helvering vs. Gregory*, that "[a]nyone may so arrange his affairs that his taxes shall be as low as possible; he is not bound to choose that pattern which will best pay the Treasury; there is not even a patriotic duty to increase one's taxes."

Many people think that income tax planning is cheating but that is not the case. Income tax planning is taking full advantage of the Internal Revenue Code (which is written to serve the interests of the rich because wealthy interests control how all laws are written) to your own advantage whether you are rich or poor.

The IRS is not going to advertise these techniques to you because it would work to their disadvantage to do so. Yet, these planning opportunities must be included for the rich who determine how the Code is written. The IRS is only charged with administering faithfully whatever the tax law happens to be.

Inform yourself of these tax code provisions that are geared towards the rich and take advantage of them for yourselves. You will not be saving the same sheer dollar amounts, but you will be able to minimize your income tax liability which is an entirely legal and economically worthwhile thing for you to do. Most people do not do it because it sounds like a very intimidating thing, and they think they will somehow be cheating. This is not accurate.

Chapter 27

Other Investments and Services

Real Advisers will recommend that you invest a greater than average portion of your portfolio in real estate. I describe in this book (and in our Form ADV Part 2) the asset allocation model that we typically will recommend. While we recommend that a majority of your assets be held in real estate and real estate-related assets, the need for liquidity is always present. It is necessary to plan for contingencies where you may need immediate cash. Consequently, while you can achieve leveraged returns with real estate, the disadvantage of this safe asset class is that sometimes, its liquidity (that is, how quickly an asset may be converted to cash) is severely restricted. That is the case because there is no real estate retail storefront (except the MLS) where you can go and sell your real estate. You must advertise it and hope that someone will come along and buy it. Consequently, real estate is deemed an illiquid asset class, and its illiquid nature is the reason for the three-year lockup that we usually employ. (Real Advisers also has a liquidity solution for our clients' real estate that we can tell you more about.)

While we always will emphasize real estate, we also recommend that you hold a portion of your portfolio in more liquid assets. These asset classes include the traditional offerings of typical money managers, and include public equities, debts and bonds, government backed bonds and securities, mutual funds, and ETFs. Real Advisers is licensed to help you with all of these through our managed account arrangements.

We will also seek to address all your financial needs, including business and personal insurance needs. These include health, auto, and life insurance.

Through my background in the legal industry, you will have access to attorneys and other finance professionals that can assist you with whatever your investment needs may be.

Chapter 28

Conclusion

This book is by no means exhaustive as to its subject matter. The Offer is intended to combine the guiding philosophy of Real Advisers with a gamifiable lead generation and team building tool. This will be accomplished through the creation of an app. This app will be used for client development and also for development of our downstream consultants. Our clients also can use it as a portal to their Real Advisers accounts and reporting and investments data. This will include immediate access to tax documents, including Schedule K-1s from investments and access to future investment opportunities offered through Real Advisers. Our representatives can use this app as a tool to serve their clients.

We will include access to sophisticated stock market tracking tools as well as tools and resources that are harder to find that pertain specifically to commercial real estate.

Subscribers also can be non-account holders who simply like the access to the messaging functionality and the forums as well as their access to budgeting tools and the study materials for the Series 65 test. The Series 65 is the exam that you would have to pass to be eligible to work with Real Advisers as a contractor advisor. With recent changes by the SEC to the accredited investor rules, passing the Series 65 also qualifies a person as an accredited investor without regard to their income or net worth.

The app will allow you to perform The Offer with friends on a "for fun" basis. This turns The Offer into a game. You can also use the app to make The Offer Price with an actual client prospect. When you make the payment of The Offer Price (either for fun or for real), the offeree will continue to get reminders about The Task. They can dismiss them, but these reminders will become prompts for them to submit their responses to The Task to the offeror (the Real Advisers representative).

If a representative initiates a sweepstakes (like I did through QuetzalHiloco's Facebook profile), the representative will receive all of the responses to The Task submitted by people hoping to receive The Offer. The representative can store and review the responses from applicants for The Offer through the app. We can include data analytics tools in the app to help the representative determine whether the applicant is legitimate. When you advertise free money, people will initiate scams and we inevitably will pay The Offer Price to people who secretly hold no intention of engaging Real Advisers. That is the risk of any business, that it will spend sales and marketing dollars on an ineffective campaign. This happens all the time, but we want to set up our representatives for success by using technology, identity verification systems, and other available data metrics (Facebook and LinkedIn profiles, for example) to verify legitimacy automatically.

The Offer can be gamified with your friends in another way that could yield additional useful data for Real Advisers. With The Bet, you can bet your hourly rate against someone else's at a fixed point in time. You both agree to give five hours of reflection time on your partner's responses to The Task. This betting pair sets a time after which they will check in to see if either has monetized an idea or achieved an accomplishment that is related to wealth accumulation. The pair can define the goals however they want. They can say that there must be an acquisition of an asset. Have either of you bought your first investment property? They can say that you must obtain education to win. Have either of you passed the Series 65? At the conclusion of the time set at the instigation of The Bet, they compare each other's progress with the goals. The Bet is one partner betting her hourly rate against her betting partner's. I could bet that I will pass the Series 65 before you buy your next investment property. The team/betting pair defines what constitutes winning. If the lower hourly rate wins, create a mechanism for giving a bonus payout like betting against the odds. Real Advisers could derive data from this. People comparing hourly rates could generate labor cost statistics.

The app will allow us to implement a recurring revenue model with subscription fees. We can provide initial value by attracting paying subscribers through implementation of a freemium model.

Appendix
Psychedelic Bibliography

Set forth below are links to several online bibliographies and other reference materials that provide valuable information about psychedelics and their therapeutic potential:

Multidisciplinary Association for Psychedelic Studies:
https://maps.org/resources/psychedelic-bibliography

The Heffter Research Institute:
https://www.heffter.org/study-publications/

Johns Hopkins Center for Psychedelic and Consciousness Research:
https://hopkinspsychedelic.org/index/#research

Yale Manual for Psilocybin-Assisted Therapy of Depression
https://thchalm.com/2020/11/18/yale-manual-for-psilocybin-assisted-therapy-of-depression/

www.ingramcontent.com/pod-product-compliance
Lightning Source LLC
Chambersburg PA
CBHW060824220526
45466CB00003B/966